MORE PRAISE FOR

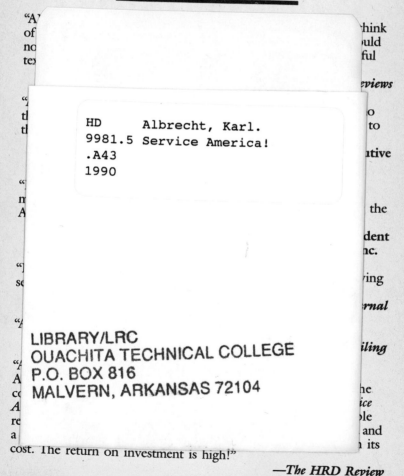

"A
of
no
te

—*eviews*

"
t
t

to

—*ative*

"
m
A

the

—dent
—nc.

"
s

—ving

—*rnal*

"

—iling

"
A
c
A
re
a

he
—ice
—le
and
—n its

cost. The return on investment is high!"

—*The HRD Review*

SERVICE ★ AMERICA!

SERVICE ★ AMERICA!

DOING BUSINESS IN THE NEW ECONOMY

KARL ALBRECHT AND RON ZEMKE

WARNER BOOKS

A Warner Communications Company

Warner Books Edition

This Warner Books edition is published by arrangement with
Dow-Jones Irwin, 1818 Ridge Road, Homewood, IL 60430

Warner Books, Inc., 666 Fifth Avenue, New York, NY 10103

Ⓦ A Warner Communications Company

Printed in the United States of America

First Warner Books Printing: June 1990

10 9 8 7 6 5 4 3 2 1

Cover design by Harold Nolan.

Library of Congress Cataloging-in-Publication Data

Albrecht, Karl.
    Service America! : doing business in the new economy / by Karl
Albrecht and Ron Zemke. — Warner Books ed.
      p.   cm.
    Reprint. Originally published: Homewood, Ill. : Dow Jones-Irwin,
c1985.
    Includes bibliographical references (p.
    ISBN 0-446-39092-5
    I. Zemke, Ron. II. Title.
HD9981.5.A43 1990
658′.00973 — dc20   90-11925
                                  CIP

PREFACE

We believe a powerful new wave is about to hit the already turbulent business world. It's the wave of *service,* or more specifically a new and intense preoccupation with the quality of service. People are getting more and more critical of the quality of service they experience in their everyday lives, and they want something done about it.

The times have changed and we no longer live in a manufacturing economy. We now live in a very new economy, a *service economy,* where relationships are becoming more important than physical products. Just as America experienced an industrial revolution around the turn of the century, so we are now experiencing a service revolution. What was once Industrial America has become Service America.

Glance around you please, and notice how much of your personal experience is involved with companies and institutions that exist for the purpose of delivering services of various kinds. Restaurants, hotels, airlines, hospitals, banks, public utilities, colleges and universities—all have the problem of gaining and retaining the patronage of their customers.

Many other organizations, such as department stores, mail-order firms, and even sellers of hard goods are finding that the invisible product—the service component—is becoming an important competitive weapon.

The times call for a new focus on service, for a number of reasons which we will explain in this book. This new *service imperative* will mean that the old customer service department will probably fade into obscurity as executives and managers work to transform their entire organizations into customer-driven business entities. The quality of the customer's experience is becoming a hot topic in board rooms and executives suites, not only in the United States but in many other countries as well. We believe this is a world-wide phenomenon.

We have tried to do several things in this book. First, of course, we want to alert forward-thinking business people, especially executives and middle managers, to the potential of this new competitive weapon of service quality. Second, we have tried to isolate some of the key factors that govern service quality, and offer examples of organizations that manage service well and of some that manage it poorly.

More important, we have tried to highlight a critical gap which we feel exists in current management thinking, namely the lack of a consistent model or framework for managing service. As a result of our experiences with many different kinds of organizations and considerable research into the operation of effective service enterprises, we have discovered an approach that we believe can help managers think about their businesses in a new and effective way. This *service management concept* is the principal contribution we hope to make with this book.

Before you read what we have to say about the management of service, it may be fair for us to declare certain points of view, so you will know what biases we bring to this subject. First, as a result of working in and with organizations, we are biased to believe that high-quality service at the front line has to start with a concept of service that exists in the minds of top management. This service concept must find its way into the structure and operation of the organization. There must be a customer-oriented culture in the organization, and it is the leaders of the enterprise who must build and maintain this culture.

We also believe in the value and importance of measuring service. An intimate and objective knowledge of how you are doing—in the customer's eyes—is critical. Market research, the service audit, and a process for measuring service quality and feeding back this information to the frontline people are crucial ingredients in moving an organization to a high level of service orientation.

We believe that *management itself is a service,* and that this point of view will become more and more prevalent as competition gets tougher and service becomes more and more a competitive weapon. Managers need to see their roles in the context of helping service people do their jobs better. The role of management in a service-driven organization is to enhance the culture, set expectations of quality, provide a motivating climate, furnish the necessary resources, help solve problems, remove obstacles, and make sure high-quality job performance pays off.

We believe this new era of service management will call for a return to the most fundamental principles of leadership and in many cases to a rethinking of the organization's basic reasons for being. Those leaders who fail to grasp the real significance of service quality will face tough times. Those who do will see their organizations thrive and prosper.

Karl Albrecht
Ron Zemke

CONTENTS

SERVICE ★ AMERICA!

1

The Service Imperative

McDonald's has more employees than U.S. Steel.
Golden arches, not blast furnaces,
symbolize the American economy.
— *George F. Will*

Ours is a service economy, and it has been one for some time. Trend analyst John Naisbitt marks the beginning of this new period as the year 1956, when, "for the first time in American history, white-collar workers in technical, managerial, and clerical positions outnumbered blue-collar workers. Industrial America was giving way to a new society."

Naisbitt labeled this new era the "information society." Earlier, Harvard sociologist Daniel Bell noted the same events and trends, and pronounced us entered into the "postindustrial society." Call it what you will, the fact remains that we live in an America, perhaps in a world and time, dominated by industries that perform rather than produce.

According to the U.S. Department of Commerce, the forecast for the foreseeable future can be summed up in four words: more of the same. There will be continued fast growth in service industries and service jobs, with data processing and hospitality leading the way. Service is no longer an industrial by-product, a sector that generates no wealth but "simply moves money around," as one economist has scoffed. Service has become a powerful economic engine in its own right—the fast track of the new American economy. *Newsweek* columnist George F. Will summarized the look of this new economy succinctly when he observed that "McDonald's has more employees than U.S. Steel. Golden arches, not blast furnaces, symbolize the American economy." We are only beginning to understand the significance of this change in the way we live and work.

Let's be clear here. We aren't suggesting that U.S. Steel is about to convert its factories into laundries to survive, or that Chrysler Corp. should consider abandoning automobile manufacturing for condominium management. As Wharton School management professor Russell Ackoff has argued, this shift toward a service-centered economy does not mean that fewer goods will be produced and consumed, "any more than the end of the agricultural era meant that fewer agricultural products were produced and consumed. *What it does mean* is that fewer people will be required to produce manufactured goods."[1] To us, that implies the gold and the growth are in services. That's where the jobs are; that's where the energy is; that's where the opportunities will continue to be.

We are persuaded that a real and important shift is under way. The fabric of our economy and the way we do business in this country are changing. This change in thrust, this transformation from a marketplace focused on goods to one focused on services, this phenomenon that Ackoff calls the "second industrial revolution" and Naisbitt refers to as the "beginning of the information society," is real and important. It is our new competitive edge—both domestically and in the world at large. Already 20 percent of the world's need for services is filled by American exports. It is only a beginning.

We contend, however, that this shift from products to services, if it is to be fully leveraged as a driving force, requires a parallel transformation in the way organizations are conceptualized, structured and, most important, managed. We contend that organizations that place a premium on the design, development, and delivery of services are as different from traditional industrial organizations as the factory is from the farm. The distinction applies not only to organizations that market pure service products (the traditional service industries) but also to manufacturers of hard goods and commodities which place a high strategic value on service and treat it as an integral part of the product they deliver. Whether service is valued simply because it is a useful strategy for product differentiation, or because service is an ingrained organizational belief, the result is the same. In those organizations service isn't a function or a department. To them, service *is* product.

SERVICE IS . . .

What do we mean by service? Several things. Bureaucrats and economists traditionally have talked about the "service sector" and defined it as consisting of "industries whose output is intangible." To the Census Bureau and the Department of Commerce, that definition covers organizations that employ just short of 60 percent of all the people employed in the United States, and applies to four broad segments of the economy:

- Transportation, communications, and utilities.
- Wholesale and retail trade.
- Finance, insurance and real estate.
- Services—the fastest growing part of the "service sector," which includes business services such as accounting, engineering, and legal firms; personal services such as housekeeping, barbering, and recreational services; and most of the nonprofit areas of the economy.

All four of these groups offer service in the classic "Help Me" sense: help me with my taxes, help me get from point A to point B, help me find a house, help me pick out a new pair of shoes. There is nothing intrinsically wrong with this traditional approach to defining who is and who isn't in the service business. It does, however, mask the full impact of service in today's marketplace.

Management expert and social scientist Peter Drucker is even more emphatic that the term *services*, as used to describe the largest portion of our contemporary economy, is a singularly unhelpful description. In a recent column in *The Wall Street Journal*, he surveys the world economy, the slump in commodity prices, and the slow recovery of manufacturing compared to the rapid growth of the service sector and states:

> We may—and soon—have to rethink the way we look at economics and economies, and fairly radically. "Information" is now classed as "services," a 19th-century term for "miscellaneous." Actually it is no more services than electrical power (which is also classed under services). It is the primary material of an information-based economy. And in such an economy the schools are as much primary producers as the farmer—and their productivity perhaps more crucial. The same in the engineering lab, the newspaper and offices in general. (January 9, 1985)

We heartily agree with Drucker's argument that service, as we know it today, is very much a primary product. It is, indeed, this argument that service is not a single-dimensioned "thing" that is at the core of our contention that service is as much a commodity as an automobile and as much in need of management and systematic study.

Harvard Business School professor Theodore Levitt agrees that the service and nonservice distinction becomes less and less meaningful as our understanding of service increases. "There are no such things as service industries. There are only industries whose service components are greater or less than those of other industries. Everybody is in service," he writes. At Citibank, half of the organization's 52,000 employees work in back rooms, never seen or heard by the public. They spend their time writing letters of credit, opening lockboxes, processing transactions, and scrutinizing everything done by the public contact people. Is Citicorp any less a manufacturer than International Business Machines Corp.? And is IBM, half of whose 340,000 employees deal directly with the public, any less a service provider? Service is everybody's business.

"FIX IT" SERVICE

The second dimension—after "Help Me" service—is service in the "Fix It" sense. It sometimes seems we are a nation of broken toys. The car is in the shop, the phone is out of order, and this computer you sold me isn't working so well either. Service in this sense is underaccounted for in the economy and marketplace, but seldom undervalued in the eye of the contemporary consumer.[2] The quality of a company's "Fix It" service is already a significant factor in its marketplace success. The capacity of an IBM, a General Electric (GE), or a Caterpillar Tractor to deliver high-quality "Fix It" service as a matter of routine—while others offer excuses, complex requirements, or failure—sets each apart in its industry and in the marketplace as a whole. We are not suggesting, of course, that manufactured goods have never before needed fixing. Far from it. But only recently have so many products become too complex for users to repair and maintain on their own. At the same time, consumers have come to expect—to demand really—that a manufacturer's obligation to guarantee the performance of a product should extend further past the point and date of purchase than ever before.

Such changes in consumer expectations can be both a bane and a blessing. It is the growing demand for high caliber "Fix It" service in the personal computer business, falling on the deaf ears of most dealers and manufacturers, for example, that is behind the space of start-up companies, like Sorbus Service Inc. and Computer Doctor Inc., which specialize in servicing electronic products. The same demand is enticing large-computer manufacturers and the few service-savvy micro producers into the development of aggressive, third-party service subsidiaries.

And what an opportunity it is! Every day a thousand Macintoshes come rolling off the Apple Computer assembly lines in Cupertino, California, while an equal number of IBM-PCs hit the road north from Florida. If we add the 3 to 5 million "orphaned" personal computers and computer peripherals in this country (which were gear-manufactured by companies that no longer exist but owned by users who do), then the need for quality "Fix It" service in the computer area alone is staggering.

According to a study by Arthur Andersen & Co. for the Association of Field Service Managers, the repair of information processing, telecommunications, and other diverse electronic products—dubbed the "electronic products service business" in the study—bills $20 billion annually, and this figure should grow to $46 billion a year by 1990.[3] Yet few manufacturers of high-tech gear are interested in the opportunities presented by this obvious void. This is so despite the fact that a well-run service operation can, by Andersen's estimates, contribute as much as 30 percent to a manufacturer's revenues. Is it any mystery that the few companies which do see the handwriting on the wall—TRW Inc., Control Data, Bell & Howell Co., Western Union Telegraph Co.—are doubling their efforts to establish solid reputations and names for themselves in the service end of the electronic future while others are content only to manufacture?

This naiveté about the value of service among producers of hard goods may be glaringly obvious in the personal-computer world, but it is hardly confined to that world. Automobile manufacturers, big steel companies, machine-tool builders and any number of consumer-product producers have suffered the same malady in the past. The attitude plainly has been, "This would be a great business if it weren't for all the damned customers." Such an attitude almost always proves to be a costly error in judgement, but it's becoming a more deadly mistake every day. Service, it increasingly turns out, can play a significant role in the economic well-being of an organization that produces hard goods. When *your* food processor is distinguishable from the competition's food processor by only a dime's worth of detailing and a dollar on the price tag, your customer service and service reputation become a critical discriminator. The GE commercial that promises, "We don't desert you after we deliver it" plucks a heartstring in a million frustrated consumers. You can count on GE.

An unusually incisive set of studies of consumer complaint

behavior was carried out during the Carter Administration for the White House Office of Consumer Affairs by a Washington, D.C., company called Technical Assistance Research Programs, Inc. (TARP). These studies spoke volumes about the positive economics of first-class service.[4] According to their findings, manufacturing organizations that don't just "handle" dissatisfied customers but go out of their way to encourage complaints and remedy them, reap significant rewards.

Among TARP's key findings are the following:

- The average business never hears from 96 percent of its unhappy customers. For every complaint received, the average company in fact has 26 customers with problems, 6 of which are "serious" problems.
- Complainers are more likely than noncomplainers to do business again with the company that upset them, even if the problem isn't satisfactorily resolved.
- Of the customers who register a complaint, between 54 and 70 percent will do business again with the organization if their complaint is resolved. That figure goes up to a staggering 95 percent if the customer feels that the complaint was resolved quickly.
- The average customer who has had a problem with an organization tells 9 or 10 people about it. Thirteen percent of people who have a problem with an organization recount the incident to more than 20 people.
- Customers who have complained to an organization and had their complaints satisfactorily resolved tell an average of five people about the treatment they received.

If automobile industry studies are correct that a brand-loyal customer represents a lifetime average revenue of at least $140,000, then the image of a manufacturer or dealer in a bitter dispute with a customer over an $80 repair bill or a $40 replacement part is plainly ludicrous. Similar logic holds for almost every business sector. In banking, the average customer represents $80 a year in profit. Appliance manufacturers figure brand loyalty is worth $2,800 over a 20-year period. Your local supermarket is counting on you for $4,400 this year and $22,000 for the five years you live in the same neighborhood.

As TARP president John Goodman put it in an address to the Nippon Cultural Broadcasting Company in Tokyo:

The fundamental conclusion [of our studies] is that a customer is worth more than merely the value of the purchase a complaint concerns. A customer's worth includes the long-term value of both the revenue and profit stream from all his purchases. This becomes particularly important if the customer could potentially purchase a range of different products from the same company.[5]

The Japanese, by the way, are only beginning to see service as important *and* problematic. Decades of concentration on manufacturing quality products and exporting finished goods have left service basically unattended to. The tendency in Japan is, as it has been here, to equate service with servitude and face-to-face attention rather than with customer-centered management.

The pattern of consumer behavior TARP uncovered is as true for industrial sales as for retail sales. There really is no mystery, then, as to why a heads-up company like Procter & Gamble prints an 800 number on all 80 of its products. This year, P & G, the nation's largest producer of consumer products (Ivory soap, Folger's coffee, Crest toothpaste, Pamper's disposable diapers, Tide detergent, and so on), expects to answer more than 750,000 telephone calls and letters from customers. A third of these replies will deal with complaints of all kinds, including those about products, ads, and even the plots of soap operas sponsored by the company. If only half of those complaints are about a product with a 30-cent margin, and only 85 percent are handled to the customer's satisfaction, the benefit to the company in the year, according to a formula developed by TARP, could exceed half a million dollars. Such a sum represents a return on investment (ROI) of almost 20 percent. The "Fix It" dimension of service is most surely an important economic force in its own right.

VALUE-ADDED SERVICE

The third service dimension shaping the way we do business is the most intangible of all. Value-added service has the feel of simple civility when delivered in a face-to-face context, but it is more than that. When it shows itself in such an ingenious and successful product as the American Express Platinum Card, it looks like perceptive marketing.

Value-added service is more easily understood in experience than in definition; you know it when you see it. Because a cabin attendant pushing the drink wagon on Republic 507 out of Chicago is out of loose change, she gives you back three one-dollar bills from a five for a $2.50 drink. In response to an off-hand comment you made, a calling officer from Wachovia Bank and Trust, who pitched factoring services to you last week, sends you an article on how to use limited trusts to help put your kids through college. A 3M visual-products representative setting up a seminar on how to use overhead projectors in sales presentations stays to help one of your salespeople rehearse for a next-day presentation. All those people are practicing the fine art of value-added service.

Each variation on the same theme is an example from, and an integral part of, the service revolution. The common thread is customer-focused service. None of these examples represents a new definition of what service means. It is rather the value and power they have in the marketplace that is new.

John Naisbitt's "high-tech/high-touch" concept has a lot to do with the development of this need. As new technology is introduced into our society, there is a counterbalancing human response. For example, Naisbitt points out, "The high technology of heart transplants and brain scanners led to a new interest in the family doctor and neighborhood clinics." In that same vein we have noticed that the advent of automated tellers in banking gave rise to a countermand by many for access to a personal banker. The more we are faced with high tech, the more we want high touch. The fewer contacts we have with the *people* of an organization, the more important the *quality* of each contact becomes. All contacts with an organization are a critical part of our perceptions and judgments about that organization. The quality of the *people contacts,* however, are often the firmest and most lasting.

Russell Ackoff sees another dimension to the demand for value-added service: a shifting focus from concern for one's standard of living toward a concern for the quality of life. If some aspects of this phenomenon represent a shift away from materialism and the "I-can-have-it-all" credo, as some claim, other factors that fall under the quality-of-life umbrella certainly signal that with a secure standard of material life, the accessories become more important. A young person's need for a car gives way to a desire for the "right kind" of automobile. Access to discretionary funds sufficient to support frequent air travel gives way to a desire for first-class seating and the best possible amenities. The total experience of obtaining a product or service becomes integrated into a real and palpable quality of the product or service itself.

Warren Blanding, editor and publisher of *Customer Service Newsletter*, suggests that several forces are at work here. Together they create a new understanding of service:

> The trend toward consumerism, the changing competitive climate and the recent recession all have forced companies to reexamine their relationships with customers. As a result, customer service has become a strategic tool. It used to be regarded as an expense. Now it is seen as a positive force for increasing sales—and for reducing the cost of sales.

The constant quest for improvement in the quality of life is not a new phenomenon, only a new mass phenomenon. In the early industrial era of this country, only the wealthy few played tennis, summered in the mountains, or wintered in the Bahamas. Today these are mass cultural experiences. Our parents and grandparents were tickled to have a paid week off, once a year. The paid vacation was a great labor victory. We—or at least some of us—jet to London for a long weekend of shopping and theater in an almost casual manner. As the mass demand for a product or service increases, the ability to deliver it effectively, efficiently, and dependably is taxed. It must be managed. Thus we find ourselves entering the service management era, the age of *systematically* designed, developed, and delivered services.

SERVICE AS A MANAGED ENDEAVOR

Historically, the terms *service* and *management* haven't rested easily side by side. Service delivery was something most self-respecting business school graduates shunned—with the exception perhaps of rising young bank officers. The concept of management seemed to encourage an orderly image antithetical to service in the traditional "Help Me" sense.

Ronald Kent Shelp, vice president of American International Group (a New York–based multinational insurance company) and chairman of the federal advisory committee on service industries, attributes those perceptions to a confusion of *personal services*— such as those provided by housekeepers, barbers, and plumbers— with the concept of *service as the provision of intangible products in general.* Consequently, service has been misperceived as always involving a one-to-one relationship between provider and receiver, as labor-intensive, and as having productivity characteristics not readily increased by capital and technology.

Characterizing service in today's economy as servitude is as inaccurate as calling Francis C. Ronney, Jr., head of Melville Corp. (the $4 billion-a-year retail chain store conglomerate that started as Thom McAn), a shoe clerk. Today two thirds of the gross national product result from service production; and at the same time, personal service in the traditional sense accounts for less than 1 percent of all service jobs. Here is how Shelp sees it:

> While personal-service jobs were declining, industrialization was calling forth a whole range of new services. Some of these were the result of new found affluence, as more and more people could afford more and better health care, education, amusement, and recreation. Other services were needed to increase the productivity of production—wholesale trade, information processing, financial services, communications. These services and others like them (engineering, consulting, retailing and insurance) became highly productive when modern technology supplied them with computers, satellite and other rapid communications, and systems analysis.
>
> Thus service jobs moved away from the low end of the economic spectrum toward the other extreme. Much of the service-oriented job growth in advanced nations has taken place in professional, managerial, administrative, and problem-solving categories. Increasingly, education became the name-of-the-game in service jobs.[6]

This change in the nature of what a service is, leads to a situation where we see a number of quite different kinds of activities nestled under the umbrella of "service and service-related industries." Shelp sorts these into five types and suggests that each developed in response to a set of stages and parallel economic conditions through which Western society has passed and through which many developing countries are now passing.[7]

Unskilled personal service. Housekeeping services for females, military conscription for males, and street vending for both sexes are the primary type of service activity in traditional societies. Historically, these kinds of jobs have provided opportunities for excess population to become socialized into urban life. Though unskilled labor exists today in this country, it is on a very different scale. People plying the trades of housekeeping, street sweeping, janitoring, and the like do exist today, but it is more likely than not that the services they provide are through a corporation like ServiceMaster International and not on a free-lance basis. It is also most likely that these organizations call on technology and mass-production techniques to assist in the delivery of the service rather than on simple brute force. But automated or not, it is a good bet that the effort is more effectively managed.

Skilled personal services. As productivity increases in agricultural societies and production exceeds subsistence levels, industrialization and trade begin to develop. Opportunities open for the kinds of services provided by skilled artisans, shopkeepers, wholesale and retail merchants, repair and maintenance people, and clerks. The need arises for complex government and government services to support both industry and the burgeoning urban population. This is the first stage of what we described above as service in the traditional sense. Yes, these services are also very much with us today, but as is the case for unskilled services, they are now organized and managed.

Industrial services. As industry becomes competitive, the need for marketplace support services arises. Industrial services are really organized groups of highly skilled specialists. Their services are, by and large, those that cannot be provided by individual contractors. They are the services offered by legal and accounting firms, banks and insurance firms, real estate brokers and trading companies. We traditionally called such services the professions and did not consider them amenable to innovation and productivity improvement. But all that is changing. The marketing and management of "professional services," as they are termed, are becoming hot topics. The creation of accounting, health, and legal franchise operations has, in effect, industrialized the industrial services.

Mass consumer services. As wealth increases in a population, discretionary purchasing power is created. This gives rise to a consumer-service industry able to enjoy economies of scale while accommodating a growing consumer demand for discretionary services. The demand for travel has promoted growth in airlines, hotels, and auto-rental companies. The demand for dining (an average of nearly two meals a day is now consumed outside the home) both fancy and fast has led to a highly variegated restaurant industry. And the demand for entertainment has created a broad base of services from movies to professional sports. A significant increase in the health and wellness industries can be attributed to the growth of discretionary dollars as well.

High-technology business services. The introduction of microchips, lasers, satellites, bioengineering and the like create opportunities for large advances in both the creation of new services and the streamlining of existing ones. The automation of goods production, data processing, and hydroponics are creations of the special services of the knowledge worker which result in a demand for new, highly technical services. The creation of industrial robots threatens production-line jobs; at the same time, a need for skilled robotic technicians is felt. Of course, it is not a one-for-one swap. Not every job lost to automation is replaced by a skill or craft job. All the same, every job that can be done by a robot will probably soon be replaced.

Another kind of service specialist created by the new technology is the knowledge consultant. Management consultants, university researchers, and software programmers are examples of such service providers. The tasks performed by each of these specialists are highly organized, integrated, and managed. This is service in its most vital and modern sense.

From this perspective it is obvious that as a society increases in sophistication and wealth, the demand for services outweighs the demand for commodities. As discretionary time and money make their presence felt in the marketplace, the ways in which one can satisfy basic needs are most likely to increase, not the basic needs themselves. Thus the railroad has seen first the automobile and then the airplane rival it as a method of fulfilling travel needs. This means that competition for the dollars of travelers and shippers has increased both within and across industries. And *increased competition,* as Shelp notes, leads to an *increased demand* for services that create efficiencies which are the basis of effective competition. At every stage of the evolution of service, we see an increase in competition among service providers as well as an increased need to effectively and efficiently deliver such services. Increased also is the awareness that a service is managed differently than a commodity.

The idea that service is a unique product that has to be understood and managed differently from a manufactured commodity isn't news to everyone. In July 1984 a *Business Week* feature, "Service as a Marketing Edge," hailed the upgrading of service from an onerous corporate chore to an important organizational strategy. Though the article focused primarily on the value-added dimension of service and not on service as a product per se, the title alone had implications that, we believe, will echo through the economy for years.

Louis V. Gerstner, Jr., newly-named president of American Express, calls service his "most strategic marketing weapon." Though the 1984 tab for the communications lines, computers, data banks, salaries, and training that went into Am Ex's service centers ran to $150 million, the benefits in terms of customer satisfaction and market information are almost incalculable. Am Ex, along with companies like P & G, IBM, Sony, General Electric, and Whirlpool, is finding that service is an active marketing tool. Such companies are learning that aggressive service programs effectively allow them to discover the demographics of their marketplace, problems with new products, customer concerns and needs, the life expectancies of their products, the ability of consumers to effect their own repairs, and the potential of proposed new products.

At Procter & Gamble, the customer-service unit at the end of the 800 number not only acts as a problem solver and value-added service to consumers but is also an effective data trap for information that can lead to other service improvements. During the 1960s, for example, P & G noticed that the average household's weekly laundry increased from 6.4 to 7.6 loads. At the same time the average wash temperature dropped 15 degrees. Closer investigation revealed that the cause of this was a multitude of new fabrics, especially synthetics, requiring closer sorting and control of the weekly wash. The upshot for P & G was the creation of the All-Temperature Cheer laundry detergent, a product especially developed to solve another of consumers' ever evolving needs.

Over the years P & G's phone lines gathered information that has led the company to develop many value-added services. On the basis of such hot-line data, the company now includes special cooking instructions for Duncan Hines brownies intended for distribution at high altitudes. It has added instructions for turning the average white cake into a wedding cake, and developed guidelines for defrosting Downy liquid fabric softner, which sometimes freezes in snow-belt states. G. Gibson Carey, a P & G advertising executive, has an explanation for the company's "knock-yourself-out-for-the-customer" approach to service that tells us something about both P & G, and value-added service in general: "There is a whole lot of enlightened self-interest in this."

Managers in such mature industries as machine tools, chemicals, consumer durables, and electronics as well as purveyors of formerly regulated services such as banking, communications, and air transportation are facing challenges that require them to take a new look at the service dimensions of their products. Traditional goods purveyors are finding that the classic market-differentiation strategies of price, quality, and special features are not enough to ensure either customer satisfaction or repeat business.

Theodore Levitt likens the relationship between today's buyer and seller to a marriage. He observes that if the act of selling someone something was once a simple, "time-discrete, bare human interaction," it is most certainly not that today. Today's buyer, whether a purchaser of industrial or consumer products, expects significantly more from the seller than a "take-the-money-and-run" attitude. As Levitt puts it:

> Buyers of automated machinery (for example) do not, like buyers at a flea market, walk home with their purchases and take their chances. They expect installation services, application aids, parts, post-purchase repair and maintenance, retrofitted enhancements, and vendor R & D to keep the products effective and up to date for as long as possible and to help the company stay competitive.
>
> Thanks to increasing interdependence, more and more of the world's economic work gets done through long term relationships between sellers and buyers. It is not a matter of just getting and then holding onto your customers. It is more a matter of giving the buyers what they want. Buyers want vendors who keep promises, [and] who'll keep supplying and standing behind what they promised. The era of the one-night stand is gone. Marriage [between buyer and seller] is both necessary and more convenient. Products are too complicated, repeat negotiations too much of a hassle and too costly. Under these conditions, success in marketing is transformed into the inescapability of a relationship.[8]

Service, in the context discussed by Levitt, is an ongoing relationship between buyer and seller that focuses on keeping the buyer happy with the seller after the sale. This is a relationship undertaken not for vague public-image purposes, but for vital economic ones. The buyer-seller relationship is not a simple contract of trust between two individuals but a promise of continuing contact between two economic entities for mutual benefit. In Levitt's words:

> During the era we are entering the emphasis will be on systems contracts, and buyer-seller relationships will be characterized by continuous contact and evolving relationships to effect the systems. The "sale" will be not just a system but a system over time. The value at stake will be the advantages of that total system over time.[9]

Levitt's point is stated in simpler terms by Bill Gove, a motivational speaker who tells the following story about a businessman named Harry, the owner of a small general-appliance store in Phoenix, Arizona:

> Harry is accustomed to being price-shopped by young couples look-ing for their first new refrigerator or washer-dryer or air conditioner. When a young couple comes into the store, pen and paper in hand, asking detailed questions about prices, features, and model numbers, Harry is pretty sure that their next move will be to trot off to a nearby discount appliance dealer to compare tags. When, after spending half an hour with such a couple and patiently answering all their questions, Harry suggests an order, he usually gets a firm, "We want to look around some other places." His rebuttal is to nod, smile, move up close, and deliver this little speech:

> "I understand that you are looking for the best deal you can find. I appreciate that because I do the same thing myself. And I know you'll probably head down to Discount Dan's and compare prices. I know I would.

> "But after you've done that, I want you to think of one thing. When you buy from Discount Dan's you get an appliance. A good one. I know because he sells the same appliances we do. But when you buy the same appliance here, you get one thing you can't get at Dan's: you get me. I come with the deal. I stand behind what I sell. I want you to be happy with what you buy. I've been here 30 years. I learned the business from my Dad, and I hope to be able to give the business over to my daughter and son-in-law in a few years. So you know one thing for sure: when you buy an appliance from me, you get me with the deal, and that means I do everything I can to be sure you never regret doing business with me. That's a guarantee." With that, Harry wishes the couple well and gives them a quart of ice cream in appreciation for their interest.

"Now," Gove asks his audience, "how far away do you think that young couple is going to get, with Harry's speech ringing in their ears and a quart of vanilla ice cream on their hands, in Phoenix, in August, when it's 125 degrees in the shade?"

Yes, it's a salesman's story, where the salesman gets cute and gets the order. But the point is exactly the same as Levitt's. Today the buyer-seller relationship is more than a fleeting, face-to-face encounter. The product purchased isn't simply an item with a set, intrinsic value the buyer is invited to take or leave. It is rather a *bundling* of the item: the product, the seller, the organization the seller represents, the service reputation of the selling organization, the service personnel, the buyer, the organization he represents, and both organizations' images in the marketplace.

Service is a key differentiation in such a marketplace, especially when the choice is among products distinguishable along no other dimension meaningful to the customer. Let's assume that you tell us that your microcomputer is better than the competitor's microcomputer because yours has a 32-bit microprocessor. But if we don't know a microprocessor from a food processor, and you don't do anything to help us see why that just might be important, then we are left not having the faintest idea why we should buy from you instead of the competitor. Or worse yet, if you tell us that your microcomputer has a 32-bit microprocessor and that *everyone's* microcomputer has a 32-bit microprocessor, you merely convince us that there isn't a dime's difference between yours and the competitor's. Let's assume you tell us that should anything go wrong with your computer—heaven forbid—a technician will be Johnny-on-the-spot in less than two hours to remedy the problem. By way of contrast, if something happens to the competitor's computer, we'll have to put it in a box and mail it back to the factory. If you then add that the factory closed up last week, you will have told us quite a lot about your computer that differentiates it from the competitor's.

Service is not *a* competitive edge, it is *the* competitive edge. People do not just buy things, they also buy expectations. One expectation is that the item they buy will produce the benefits the seller promised. Another is that if it doesn't, the seller will make good on the promise. When a company picks Xerox Corporation over Canon Inc. as a photocopy machine supplier, many considerations go into the decision. One is the dependability of the "Fix It" service reputation that accompanies the Xerox name. If the technician providing the "Fix It" service maintains the machine in line with the buyer's expectations, and does so in a way that gives an impression of competence and friendliness, the relationship is solidified along two additional dimensions. Should the technician prove to be either incompetent or offensive to the buyer's employees in the fulfillment of his duties, the relationship may be short-lived despite the fact that the initial conditions of the decision have not changed.

Let's consider why IBM's personal computer sells so well when a multitude of cheaper yet similar computers are available, and when the market contains several competitors, notably the Wang personal computer and Apple's Macintosh, that seemingly offer so much more of a machine for the same money? Indeed, why does IBM do so well in the *big* computer business when companies like NCR Corporation, Amdahl, and Tandem sell mainframe computers said to be faster, better, more reliable, and better maintained than IBM's?

To answer this question, we have to go back to the young couple at Harry's appliance store in Phoenix. If they can afford the purchase, they will return to Harry's to buy their air conditioner. When you buy from Harry, you buy from the best. And if anything goes wrong, you can rely on good old Harry. In the same way, when you buy from IBM, you don't just get a computer, you get IBM with the deal—a value of considerable weight in any purchase decision. If the buyer buys and the computer doesn't work, there is no second guessing: "Hey, what more could we do? We went with IBM." IBM doesn't just design, build, and deliver the product; IBM *is* the product. And IBM says so, just as loudly and as often as it can. And we get the message.

While most business schools still teach an approach to management and management science more appropriately described as "industrial management," this situation is changing today. The stunning success of corporations like McDonald's, Federal Express, ServiceMaster Industries, and ARA Services—all companies whose products are almost purely services—has caused academics, entrepreneurs, and eager business school graduates to look at service industries with a new respect. Those organizations, which are among the most profitable and fastest growing in the country, could never have achieved the results they have achieved without highly competent, sophisticated management. Managers in such companies as well as in financial services organizations like American Express, Citicorp, Phibro-Salomon, Allied Bancshares, and Dun & Bradstreet, as well as retailers like Wal-Mart, Melville, Super Valu Stores, Southland, Lucky Stores, and Dayton-Hudson are proving that service is both big business and a challenge to the most demanding of management minds.[10]

THE SERVICE MANAGEMENT CHALLENGE

Economics and sociology have conspired. Carl Sandburg's "Stormy, husky, brawling, City of Big Shoulders"—Chicago, which was America's "Hog Butcher for the World, Tool Maker, Stacker of Wheat, Player with Railroads"—is but a romantic memory today. Service is now the business of business in America.

The capacity to serve customers effectively and efficiently is an issue every organization must face. No one can evade this challenge: manufacturers and traditional service providers, profit-making and nonprofit organizations, private-sector and public enterprises must all face the task of responding effectively and efficiently to customers and consumers who expect quality and service as a part of every purchase. Some organizations are well aware of this need and have responded to it. For others, the need to be customer-focused and service-preoccupied comes as a rude surprise. But it cannot be ignored; it is not a momentary fad that will suddenly go away. It is the new standard used by customers and consumers to measure organizational performance. Increasingly, the marketplace is opting to do business with those who serve, and declining involvement with those who merely supply.

Organizations concerned with honing a competitive edge for the 1980s, 90s, and beyond must develop two new capacities. The first is the ability to think strategically about service and to build a strong service orientation around and into the vision of their strategic future. The second capacity, which is perhaps more difficult to develop, is the ability to effectively and efficiently manage the design, development, and delivery of service. In our view the ability to manage the production and delivery of a service differs from the ability to manage the production and delivery of a commodity. It requires a familiarity with the idea of an intangible having economic value, and a deftness in conceptualizing *intangible* outcomes. It requires a tolerance for ambiguity, an ease in dealing with lack of direct control over every key process, and a finely tuned appreciation of the notion that the organization is equally dependent on soft (or people-related) skills and hard (or production-related) skills. Last but not least, it requires a tolerance for—perhaps even an enjoyment of—sudden and sometimes dramatic change. The only constant in service is change.

Not all individuals and organizations are up to this challenge. Some take to it like ducks to water. In between, are those individuals and organizations who can, and eventually will, master the art and science of managed service delivery. It is our hope that what follows—our account of how others have met and mastered the challenge, and the principles we have extracted from their success—will make this mastery easier.

2

What We Can Learn about Service from Scandinavia

We have 50,000 moments of truth out there every day.
—*Jan Carlzon, president, Scandinavian Airlines*

SWEDEN AS A BELLWETHER COUNTRY

It's interesting to trace the diffusion of ideas around the world. Something germinates in one place and is carried to another place largely by the accidents of human contact. Like seeds borne in the fur of wandering animals, ideas often pass from person to person and from culture to culture. The channels of commerce have for many years provided an infrastructure for the movement of ideas.

Some futurists believe that the most socially provocative ideas tend to originate in certain areas of the world more than others— especially is this the case for Scandinavia. According to Marvin Cetron and Thomas O'Toole, authors of *Encounters with the Future,* Sweden in particular seems to be the current bellwether nation. They believe that "for most of the 20th century, social change has come first to Sweden and then swept through the rest of Scandinavia before coming to America." They view Sweden, Denmark, and Norway as cultural settings more conducive to social innovation than most other countries.

This generalization may be a bit too broad, but it does seem to have a certain credibility to it. Many people think of Sweden as the starting point for unorthodox ideas about sexual relationships, with the much publicized "trial marriage" a case in point. Books and films from Sweden tend to capture the attention of the literati in America and to represent ideas that seem ahead of their time. Some thinkers in the United States health care industry study Swedish hospitals as examples of the best—and the worst—of socialized delivery systems. Swedish military concepts take novel approaches, such as designing fighter planes that can land on highways, if necessary. Swedish cars tend toward advanced technical designs rather than those that are merely cosmetic.

Scandinavian countries may simply place a higher value on social experimentation than do other nations. Or perhaps we assume this to be so and see what we expect to see. In any case, it is instructive to see what's happening there in the area of service. Do the Scandinavian countries pay more attention to the quality of customer service than others? Do they tend to design their commercial systems around human experience more than, say, Americans do?

To answer that question, let's go back to about 1980. We would like to trace the Scandinavian origins of a conceptual approach to service that we think will have enormous significance in the business world, not only in America but around the world. While we in the United States were busy talking about managing in a service economy. the Scandinavians figured out how to do it.

NOT ANOTHER JAPANESE MANAGEMENT THEORY!

In case you're one of the people who have been bombarded by the slogans of Japanese management over the past few years, we offer a bit of assurance. What follows is not a clarion call for a new management panacea—we are not offering to substitute herring for sushi. But we do think the Swedes, Danes, and Norwegians deserve substantial credit for their achievements in the design, development, and delivery of service. What follows is a story we find intriguing. We believe it holds the seeds of an idea whose time may well have come in America, and we suspect in much of the rest of the Western business world.

THE SAS STORY

In 1981, Scandinavian Airlines System—SAS as it is known in the industry—was struggling with a severe downturn in business; this was true of virtually all other airlines as well. The worldwide recession had cut deeply into the airline industry, and companies were bleeding from every pore. During that year SAS posted an $8 million loss.

The multinational board of directors of SAS was understandably concerned. The company president resigned and the board promoted to that position a young superstar, Jan Carlzon. An energetic, flamboyant man of 39, Carlzon had been managing one of the company's subsidiaries. He had a strong marketing orientation, which became his strongest asset in the turnaround struggle that was to come.

While most other airline companies were whittling back their expenditures with an energy bordering on desperation, Carlzon decided to go in exactly the opposite direction. He embarked on a virtual death-or-glory expedition to turn SAS around, and his strategy revolutionized the company's attitude toward its customers.

What followed was a spectacularly successful turnaround maneuver in which SAS went from the $8 million loss figure to a *gross profit of $71 million* on sales of $2 billion in a little over a year. SAS was voted "airline of the year" and laid claim to being the most punctual airline in Europe. The company strove for, and largely achieved, recognition as "the businessman's airline."

All of this happened in a remarkably short span of time while the rest of the airline industry was losing an aggregate of $1.7 billion per year.

HOW SAS DID IT

Naturally, more than a few people were curious to know just how Carlzon had managed to pull that particular rabbit out of his hat. Carlzon did not attribute his success to such conventional tactics as advertising, rate cutting, and cost reduction—or even to his own leadership. He credited most of the improvement to the effects of a deceptively simple philosophy of marketing: *make sure you're really selling what the customer wants to buy.*

"Look," Carlzon began to say to everyone in the company who would listen, "for too many years we've been production-oriented. We've been putting almost all our attention on the mundane aspects of flying airplanes, and not enough on the quality of the customer's experience. It's time we as a company shifted the focus of our attention. Our business is not flying airplanes, it's serving the travel needs of our public. If we can do that better than the other companies, we'll get the business. If we can't, we won't get the business and we don't deserve to."

Carlzon believed that if he could teach most SAS managers

and employees to keep tabs on the kind of treatment the customer received at each of the critical stages of his or her dealings with the company, they could create a conscious impression of service quality for the customer to carry away. By "turning on" the whole organization to the mission of service, he believed he could get the customer to recognize a significant difference between SAS and all other available choices. This would bring the customer back in the future and generate goodwill that would result in a significant level of word-of-mouth business.

To explain the paradigm shift he wanted to bring about, Carlzon drew a diagram that eventually became permanently embedded in the visual memory of his managers. The diagram was a simple square figure. Each corner of the diagram contained one of the four points of emphasis in Carlzon's new approach: market, product, delivery system, and image.

In Carlzon's view SAS had become an "introverted" organization which had lost its conceptual focus on the customer's needs as critically important to success. Frontline people tended to be preoccupied with their individual tasks. Managers were concerned about routine managerial duties and administrative people about forms and reports. In such an organization, the prevailing attitude seemed to be, "If only the customers would go away and leave me alone, I could get my job done."

"Who," Carlzon asked, "is paying attention to the real needs of the customer?" He believed it was time to shift the focus of attention from the production process—the delivery system—to the market. "We must pay attention to what our customers are telling us with their behavior," he asserted. "The world is changing, business is changing, and the needs of our customers are changing. Unless we become truly a customer-driven organization, we won't grow. We must formulate a viable *concept* for service."

Carlzon contended that a constant preoccupation with the customer's motivational structure—the needs of the market—would force attitudinal and structural changes in the SAS organization. This would mean a shift in the deployment of the delivery system so that it could be more in harmony with the customer's human priorities. If that happened, Carlzon reasoned, the company's image would improve. As its image improved, its performance in the market would improve, and the process would become self-reinforcing.

With the help of his key executives, Carlzon began to preach and teach this gospel of customer orientation energetically and persistently throughout the organization, taking it right down to the front-line employees. Here we find an interesting contrast between this Scandinavian approach and the way such a program would have been carried out in the United States. The characteristic American approach to bringing a new theme down to the grassroots level would involve putting the middle managers, and perhaps the first-line supervisors as well, through a training program. It would then be hoped that the word would trickle down through the ranks of the rest of the organization. (This doesn't usually happen, of course.)

Carlzon reasoned that such a new concept would require a radical redirection of the thoughts and energies of everyone in the organization, thus requiring an inordinately long time to diffuse down through the ranks. It was not that his managers were not loyal, intelligent, or committed. He simply recognized the reality of human organizations: new ideas tend to diffuse slowly, and adaptation to new ideas tends to proceed at a snail's pace. Let's recall that we are talking here about an organization of some 20,000 people located in three countries. The managerial group alone consisted of about 120 executives, 1,750 middle managers, and 3,000 supervisors and crew chiefs.

Since Carlzon was convinced that the game would be over if he had to wait for the new gospel to "take" at its own speed, he decided to jump over the management levels and take his message directly to the working people. He formed an implementation team consisting of consultants and hand-picked executives at the highest levels. He and his team embarked on an aggressive campaign to change the thinking of some 20,000 people.

Carlzon followed through with an intensive campaign to demonstrate a philosophy he referred to simply as "visible management." He and his executives personally shouldered the task of evangelism. All executives were expected to devote a substantial portion of their time to spreading the word. In particular, they were instructed to use their personal clout as well as formal authority to direct the attention of managers at all levels to Carlzon's new gospel.

The most energetic and hard-working of all the executive evangelists was probably Carlzon himself, who personally visited frontline people all over the SAS system. In Sweden, Denmark, and Norway he preached his gospel of service, creativity, and finding a better way. He staged theatrical presentations and used highly provocative methods to put his points across.

Carlzon and his team followed through with convincing evidence of their own commitment: they put *all 20,000* SAS managers and *employees* through a two-day training program designed to help them grow as individuals and to fill them with a new and dynamic sense of the organization's purposes. They hired one of the best-known training companies in Europe, Time Manager International, which made use of a high-energy, inspirational style of training. There was also an intensive internal program of employee communications, aimed at constantly reinforcing the message.

This is not to imply that the SAS managers were ignored or left out of the process. The effort to indoctrinate them was just as intensive as that directed at the performance-level people. In fact, before launching the mass training phase, Carlzon had hosted an intensive three-week gathering of the top 120 firm executives and 30 senior union representatives.[1] Reviewing together the new approach, these executives and union representatives thought deeply about the philosophical and strategic questions involved in implementing it and discussed the developments required in various divisions of the company. Training for middle managers proceeded more or less in tandem with the frontline training. In many cases supervisors joined with performance-level people at large-group training sessions of 100 or more persons.

Certainly, SAS did much more than merely train its employees. Out of the management meetings came a number of projects and programs for putting the SAS organization back into shape. These ventures greatly helped create the public impression that something new was going on at SAS, even though Carlzon and his leaders attributed their ultimate success to a new way of thinking rather than to any specific business moves.

To strengthen the follow-through process, Carlzon set up an internal consulting group. He asked its members to work directly with managers all over the organization in an effort to find ways of overcoming obstacles and moving ahead the various projects.

Here, too, Carlzon himself took an aggressive lead in finding new ways to serve the customer. One of his brainchildren became known in-house as the BMA project—the businessman's airline. He decided that, rather than try to be all things to all people when, in fact, the company hadn't been much of anything to anybody, SAS should have a "best-known-for" feature. Its best bet was to become famous for catering to the needs of day-time business travelers moving regularly about Europe and Scandinavia.

SAS had for some time been operating a singularly illogical seat-pricing system on its regular flights. Of course, the airline industry is well known for its peculiar, often baffling price structures, but SAS's scheme outdid those of most companies. A business executive who had paid the full fare for a seat might often find himself or herself sitting beside a college student with a backpack who had paid a substantially lower fare. Should this point arise in the course of their conversation, the executive might well wonder, "Why am I paying more for my ticket, but not getting anything more for my money?" SAS marketing people soon realized that the company's image with business travelers, who contributed the lion's share of SAS's receipts, had deteriorated badly.

This led to the creation of the highly successful Euroclass service. Even for relatively short flights, a business traveler could partake of a somewhat higher level of comfort and service, and could sit in a separate curtained-off section of the cabin. This normalization of fare structures and service levels did a great deal for SAS's image in the minds of business travelers.

A second important change masterminded by Jan Carlzon was the take-off-on time program. Seeking to score points with business travelers, he decided to make SAS the most punctual airline in Europe. "Can we come up with a new plan in six months?" he asked his operating executives. "If so, how much do you think it will cost?" This challenge captured the imagination of a number of key players, and it became a sort of rallying idea.

The original estimate for the venture was a six-months' undertaking at a cost of about 8 million Swedish kronor, which is equal to about $1 million. The project won so much support at so many levels that it took only three months for SAS to become the most punctual European airline at a cost of only about 1 million kronor, which amounts to about $125,000.

Again, Carlzon's constant influence lent impetus to the effort. According to legend, he went so far as to install in his office a video showing the status of every flight in the SAS system. It was not unusual for an SAS pilot to land at his destination city and have someone hand him this message: "Mr. Carlzon would like you to call him." When the pilot dialed through, Carlzon would say, "I just wondered why your plane took off late." Perhaps there was an acceptable reason beyond normal human control, but the effect was to keep the pressure on at all levels. Few SAS pilots looked forward to the prospect of explaining to the president of the company why they didn't get their customers in the air at the advertised time.

One internal project that helped defray some of the costs of these provocative new ventures was a skillfully executed program of cost savings. Rather than simply hand down the typical decree calling for a percentage cut in budgets across the board, the implementation team launched a creative search for opportunities to do more with less. All told, SAS management put up over 250 million Swedish kronor, equivalent to over $30 million, in efforts to revolutionize the company's approach to its business. And even with that big an outlay, SAS made a dramatic turnaround into a profitable mode while its competitors were losing money.

According to Olle Stiwenius, director of the internal SAS management consultants, "Jan Carlzon really masterminded the turnabout maneuver. He had a great deal of help from many talented people, but he himself supplied the vision to get it going and the energy to see it through." Stiwenius and others describe Carlzon as possessed of two key traits that made him the right man for the times: a creative mind and the ability to communicate his expectations clearly and dramatically. He managed to get the top management of SAS to rethink the company's destiny and to come up with possibilities that enabled them to see beyond their previous conception of the business.

THE TEACHINGS OF CHAIRMAN JAN

Though Carlzon's high-profile turnaround strategy attracted considerable attention, few people understood immediately the real implications of what SAS had achieved under his guidance. What was not readily visible to the casual observer was that Carlzon had evolved, largely in an intuitive way, a unique approach to the company's management. This approach was characterized by an almost obsessive commitment to *managing the customer's experience* at all points in the cycle of service. Given this obsessive commitment as a starting point, the task became one of getting as many of the heads as possible turned in the right direction and helping them to see Carlzon's new vision of the company's place in the market.

Many management theorists in Sweden, and indeed all over Scandinavia, began to study this new management philosophy. Because of his flamboyant personality, Carlzon was seldom at a loss for words, and many of his one-liners convey a strong sense of his own attitudes toward the conduct of a service business.

A Carlzon wisecrack that caught the attention of many SAS people was, "There is nothing more rotten and useless than an airplane seat that leaves the ground empty." A more telling line that is beginning to find its way into the lexicon of business executives all over Europe was, "We have 50,000 moments of truth out there every day." A *moment of truth,* by Carlzon's definition, is an episode in which a customer comes into contact with any aspect of the company, however remote, and thereby has an opportunity to form an impression.

The problem and the challenge, from this point of view, are that most moments of truth take place far beyond the immediate line of sight of management. Since managers cannot be there to influence the quality of so many moments of truth, they must learn to manage them indirectly, that is, by creating a customer-oriented organization, a customer-friendly system as well as a work environment that reinforces the idea of putting the customer first.

SERVICE MANAGEMENT: THE EMERGENCE OF A THEORY

Management experts of various stripes all over Sweden, and indeed all over Scandinavia, began to get wind of the Carlzon adventure. Carlzon was the kind of person who was highly visible and got into the news frequently. And, after all, he had masterminded one of the most dramatic corporate turnarounds ever in Scandinavia and Europe. As the various management thinkers analyzed Carlzon's approach, they began to recognize the elements of a model. Word spread of this new approach to the management of service organizations, and a new management theory was born: *service management.*

Soon representatives of other service companies began beating a path to the door of SAS. "How did you do it?" they wanted to know. "What are the essential ingredients of service management, and how can they be implemented in our industry?" Books, articles, masters' theses, doctoral dissertations, and seminars began to appear. Service management was the new wave in Scandinavia. The term *service management* and the concept associated with it became so popular that Scandinavian management institutions and technikons began to offer concentrations in service management within the framework of business degrees. Service management became the most popular topic for top-management and middle-management seminars.

The bloom may not stay on the SAS rose forever, of course. One thing we know for sure is that success in business today does not place a guarantee on tomorrow. There is no permanent solution to the problem of excellent service performance, and what works now may not work next year. As the venerable Peter Drucker puts it, "Time has a way of changing your assets into liabilities." Attention to service needs to be a self-renewing process. It will be interesting to see how well SAS maintains its position over the years.

HOW SERVICE MANAGEMENT IS DIFFUSING

In late 1983 we discovered service management and decided to put its concepts to use in our own work. Karl Albrecht was visiting Copenhagen at the time, working with a highly creative group of Danish training consultants called Connector International. They related the SAS story and pointed out that the service management theory was rapidly gaining converts in Scandinavia. Albrecht had not previously heard of the concept, which to the best of his knowledge had not yet made an impact in America. Subsequent discussions with other management thinkers in Britain and continental Europe confirmed the fact that they knew nothing of it as well.

After Albrecht returned to the United States, both of us set about exploring the possibility of applying service management concepts in our own consulting work. As a result of many discussions and a great deal of further investigation, we concluded that service management was a story worth telling. And that led us to the decision to write this book.

The fact that service management, as we first knew it, originated in Scandinavia is not the important part of the story. What is important is that people in service businesses desperately need a *model* for thinking about service: the times call for it. This is why we believe that what we describe as service management—call it whatever you like—is an idea whose time has come.

Some Scandinavians seem to feel that the service management concept did not really originate in Scandinavia at all. In late 1984 Karl Albrecht, who was on an SAS flight from London to Stockholm in order to complete part of the research for this book, got into conversation with a Swedish businessman sitting in the next seat. "Oh, yes, we've all heard about service management," the man smiled. "But what brings you to Scandinavia to study it? I thought it all started with your Peter Drucker." It's a small world!

We should also add at this point that Scandinavian companies have no particular monopoly on excellence of service. A number of American firms have earned reputations for outstanding service and customer orientation. IBM, in particular, comes to mind here. For years IBM managers at all levels have heard the gospel of closeness to the customer preached from a variety of pulpits. The Marriott hotel chain has invested enormously in building a service image, and has managed to make it stick for the most part. The McDonald's fast-food chain has achieved a level of service embodied in its motto, "Quality, Service, Cleanliness, and Value," that is the standard of comparison for the whole fast-food industry. Walt Disney, the man who virtually invented the theme park, founded an organization that has made customer service seem so perfectly natural that experts have scrutinized Disney's employee and management training as if it might have magic incantations hidden somewhere in it.

All of these firms have at least one thing in common: a clear *model for service.* In each case, their leaders have arrived at a clear and communicable definition of excellence. This is the sine qua non—the essential first step. In each case, the individual organization has embarked on its own particular way of actualizing its service strategy, but all of them have clear strategies from which to work.

Service management makes a great deal of sense in virtually any industry that deals in an intangible product or in an industry where products are relatively indistinguishable from one another. Examples that arise immediately are airlines, banks and savings and loan associations (S&Ls), hotels, restaurants, resorts, theme parks, hospitals, public utilities, financial management organizations, educational institutions, and government service agencies. Even organizations producing highly tangible products can benefit from certain elements of the service management point of view.

As we began the detailed research for this book, we discovered the first real evidence that service management as a formal concept was diffusing out of Scandinavia into northern Europe. A very striking example is British Airways's Customer First program, which we shall describe in some detail in a later chapter. The "Brits" took a page or two out of the SAS book, but they have made the idea uniquely their own.

The British Airways's program was so successful, almost right from the start, that it captured a great deal of attention in Britain. In some ways BA may have outdone SAS in the implementation.

Other organizations in Britain and continental Europe are beginning to adopt the new philosophy of service and to transform it into their own versions.

At this point we return to our previous promise that we are neither sounding a clarion call for the next Japanese management technique nor substituting herring for sushi. This is not a book about Swedish management, Danish management, Norwegian management, or even Scandinavian management. It is a book about *service management*. We acknowledge the Scandinavian origin of the idea, and we heartily thank our colleagues there for putting us onto the conceptual track. But the idea of a customer-driven organization is a transnational idea. We don't have to import the cultural trappings of a distant society. Our job in America, and indeed the job of practitioners in all countries, is to build upon a worthwhile idea and take it for our own.

Service management is a *transformational concept*, we believe. It is a philosophy, a thought process, a set of values and attitudes, and—sooner or later—a set of methods. To transform an entire organization into a customer-oriented entity takes time, resources, planning, imagination, and an enormous *commitment by management*. The process is conceptually simple, but given the monolithic resistance to change displayed by most organizations, it is almost always a very tall order.

3

The Triangle of Service

> When the moments of truth go unmanaged, the quality of service regresses to mediocrity.
> —*Karl Albrecht/Ron Zemke*

50,000 MOMENTS OF TRUTH

The metaphor of the *moment of truth* is a very powerful idea for helping people in service businesses shift their points of view and think about the customer's experience. SAS president Jan Carlzon's one-liner, "We have 50,000 moments of truth out there every day," really hits home. Here is a case in point.

A friend of ours was traveling alone in Japan on an extended vacation. He inquired in his limited Japanese which train he should take to go from Sapporo, where he was at the moment, to Tokyo. The man behind the counter wrote out all the information for him—times, train numbers, and track numbers. He even took the trouble to write it in both English and Japanese, in case our friend should lose his way and later need to show the note to some other Japanese person.

This was a moment of truth, one of many that happened that day. At that instant our friend had an opportunity to form an impression of the train company, or at least of that one employee. He came away thinking, "That was a nice experience. There's somebody who really takes the trouble to help people."

But the story goes even a bit further. Pleased and gratified, our friend thanked the information man and walked down the corridor to the waiting area, to sit and wait for the departure time. A half-hour later he saw the information man come bustling through the crowded waiting hall, looking for him. Locating him at last, the man gestured for the return of the paper. He wrote something on it, gave it back, bowed quickly, and hurried back to his post. He had figured out a faster, more convenient sequence of trains, and came back to correct the note!

Managing service means having as many of the moments of truth as possible come out well. As Donald Porter, director of customer service quality assurance for British Airways, points out:

> If you're a service person, and you get it wrong at your point in the customer's chain of experience, you are very likely erasing from the customer's mind all the memories of the good treatment he or she may have had up until you. But if you get it right, you have a chance to undo all the wrongs that may have happened before the customer got to you. *You* really are the moment of truth.

Each of us has a personal storehouse of memories of the moments of truth in our life experiences. We have experienced lousy moments when it seemed that people or systems or both almost went out of their way to be difficult or unhelpful. And we have had shining moments when we felt appreciated, cared for, cared about, and genuinely valued.

From your point of view as the customer, or the receiver of the service, you experience the moment of truth as *intensely personal.* You think, "This is *me* standing here, not some faceless nonentity. I am a person. I have an important stake in this situation, and I want very much to be treated properly." Most of us will forgive "system" screwups, even to a preposterous degree, if there is someone there who acknowledges our personal needs and makes an effort to set things right. The concept of managing the moments of truth is the very essence of service management.

GETTING HIGH GRADES ON THE CUSTOMER'S REPORT CARD

Every time a service organization performs for a particular customer, the customer makes an assessment of the quality of the service, even if unconsciously. The sum total of the repeated assessments by this customer and the collective assessments by all customers establish in their minds the organization's image in terms of service quality.

We can think of the customer as carrying around a kind of "report card" in his or her head, which is the basis of a grading system that leads the customer to decide whether to partake of the service again or to go elsewhere. As we shall see later, it is crucially important for us to find out as much as we possibly can about this all-important but invisible report card. We can only score high grades on the customer's report card on a consistent basis by knowing what evaluation factors the customer is applying when he or she thinks about our organization and what we offer.

THE PRINCIPLE OF REGRESSION TO MEDIOCRITY

Why *don't* the trains run on time? Why is getting a telephone installed a major adventure? Why do so many people consider "postal service" a contradiction in terms? Why did C. Northcote Parkinson, the originator of the famed Parkinson's Law, claim, "If there's anything a public servant hates to do, it's something for the public"? Why is there so little perception on the part of T. C. Mits (the celebrated man-in-the-street) of quality in service? Why is outstanding service considered so scarce when so many companies presumably thrive or perish on the satisfaction of their customers? We think these questions, and others like them, can be answered in meaningful ways—ways that suggest solutions.

A story shared by Donald Porter of British Airways foreshadows the answer to the question of why service quality is so frequently low. "When we launched our Customer First campaign," Porter reports, "we wanted to find out where we were in our market at the time. What did our customers think of us, compared to other airline companies? We conducted a market research study to try to find out.

"Our study aimed at answering two questions: first, what factors did people really consider most important in their flying experiences; and second, how did British Airways stack up against the other airlines on those factors?

"After some extensive interviewing and data analysis, we discovered some very interesting facts. Of all the statements made by the air travelers we interviewed, four factors stood out from all the rest as being critically important. What took us aback was the fact that two of the four factors came more or less as a surprise to us—we hadn't really considered them consciously before."

According to BA's findings, says Porter, travelers seemed to be responding to four key factors as they moved through the chain of experience:

1. Care and concern—"We knew about this one."
2. Spontaneity—"We hadn't thought much about this one."

3. Problem solving—"We were conscious of this one."
4. Recovery—"We hadn't thought about this one at all."

" 'Care and concern' are fairly clear, I think," says Porter. "We weren't surprised to find this a key factor, although I think we'd have to confess that we couldn't claim a very high level of performance on it.

" 'Spontaneity' made us stop and scratch our heads a bit. Customers were saying, 'We want to know that your frontline people are authorized to think. When a problem comes up that doesn't fit the procedure book, can the service person use some discretion—find a way to jockey the system on the customer's behalf? Or does he or she simply shrug shoulders and brush the customer off?

" 'Problem solving' was pretty clear, we felt. Customers thought our people should be skilled at working out the intricacies of problematical travel schedules, handling complicated logistics, and in general getting them on their way.

"The fourth factor sort of threw us. It had never really occurred to us in any concrete way. 'Recovery' was the term we coined to describe a very frequently repeated concern: if something goes wrong, as it often does, will anybody make a special effort to set it right? Will someone go out of his or her way to make amends to the customer? Does anybody make an effort to offset the negative effects of a screwup? Does anyone even know how to deliver a simple apology?

"We were struck by a rather chilling thought: if two of these four primary evaluation factors were things we had never consciously considered, what were the chances that our people in the service areas were paying attention to them? For the first time, we were really beginning to understand and come to terms with the real motivational factors that are embedded in our customer's nervous system."

Porter's commentary offers a great deal to think about. The market research project also came up with some other interesting findings. When the interviewers asked air travelers to rate British Airways in comparison to other airlines they had personally dealt with, they found some interesting statistics. About 20 percent of the respondents considered British Airways superior to other airlines they had used. About 15 percent considered British Airways inferior to others. The remainder expressed no strong opinions one way or the other.

The initial reaction of company management to the figures was guardedly optimistic. One executive offered the interpretation that "it seems like 85 percent of the people interviewed think we're OK." But as the implications of the data began to soak in, the attitude changed to one of mild concern. Another observer volunteered, "There is another interpretation that one could make. It seems that 65 percent of the respondents don't see any important difference between us and the other airlines. That doesn't strike me as very good news."

This, indeed, was *bad news*, when considered in the light of a clear and specific directive from Colin Marshall, chief executive of British Airways. "I want British Airways to be *the best airline in the world,* " he said, "and I'm willing to do whatever it takes to make it that." With 65 percent of the people apparently evaluating the company as just so-so in quality of service, there seemed to be quite a distance to go.

From many of *our* everyday experiences, as well as from the British Airways case, we can draw a fairly mundane conclusion, one that we believe can be stated as an out-and-out *principle* of service management:

WHEN THE MOMENTS OF TRUTH GO UNMANAGED, THE QUALITY OF SERVICE REGRESSES TO MEDIOCRITY.

"Just a moment," you might say. "Isn't it a little harsh to define an average level of service—neither poor nor outstanding— as 'mediocre?' Isn't just 'okay' okay?"

Perhaps so, but consider that to survive and prosper in a service industry requires *differentiation.* An effective service company must show evidence that it really does have something special to offer. Especially in industries where customers don't readily see important differences in the choices of service offered them, "average" really equates to "mediocre," at least in the mind of the customer.

Porter contributes another observation on this point. "We had heard a great deal about SAS's 'punctuality' reputation. SAS made quite a noise with their adverts, telling business travelers how punctual they were. Yet, when we did our market study, we didn't find a great deal of concern about on-time takeoff.

"It seemed to us that the on-time factor had lost its significance once most of the airlines improved on it. Our customers were saying, in effect, 'Look, don't talk to us about taking off on time. We *expect* you to take off on time. Don't look for a standing ovation just because you get the thing off the ground on the published schedule.' "

The message here, we think, is that *customer expectations are progressive.* If you're accustomed to telephone service in the United States, not only will you be horrified at the "average" level of service in New Delhi but you will also tend to disapprove of short-falls in the American level of service as well, even though it is better than just about any other in the world. As customers, we tend to expect at least the level we've become used to.

Thomas Peters and Robert Waterman point out in *In Search of Excellence* the crucial importance of "staying close to the cus-tomer." By this they mean learning in intimate detail what really counts to your customer; what he or she likes and doesn't like; what the customer will and won't buy. Some of the most dismal failures of organizations can be traced to losing contact with the customer at the very time when the customer's needs and motiva-tions were changing. To paraphrase those famous last words, "There will always be a market for a good buggy whip."

SEEING SERVICE AS A PRODUCT

In addition to learning to understand the customer better, we need to understand the concept of service itself better. Though a service is obviously different from a physical product, it is still a product. A service product—any incident of *doing* for others for a fee—can be distinguished from a commodity by one or more, and usually several, of the following service characteristics:

1. A service is produced at the instant of delivery; it can't be created in advance or held in readiness.
2. A service cannot be centrally produced, inspected, stock-piled, or warehoused. It is usually delivered wherever the customer is, by people who are beyond the immediate influence of management.
3. The "product" cannot be demonstrated, nor can a sample be sent for customer approval in advance of the service; the provider can show various examples, but the custom-er's own haircut, for example, does not yet exist and can-not be shown.
4. The person receiving the service has nothing tangible; the value of the service depends on his or her personal experience.

5. The experience cannot be sold or passed on to a third party.
6. If improperly performed, a service cannot be "recalled." If it cannot be repeated, then reparations or apologies are the only means of recourse for customer satisfaction.
7. Quality assurance must happen before production, rather than after production, as would be the case in a manufacturing situation.
8. Delivery of the service usually requires human interaction to some degree; buyer and seller come into contact in some relatively personal way to create the service.
9. The receiver's expectations of the service are integral to his or her satisfaction with the outcome. Quality of service is largely a subjective matter.
10. The more people the customer must encounter during the delivery of the service, the less likely it is that he or she will be satisfied with the service.

Note please that we are not suggesting that every service can or should possess every one of these ten characteristics—or even that these are the only characteristics a service can have. Just the same, these characteristics paint a picture of a very special kind of transaction between buyer and seller: the transaction we call service. The more we understand this transaction, the higher the grades we can earn on the customer's report card.

THE CYCLE OF SERVICE

One of the obvious places to start in thinking about the quality of an organization's service is to take inventory of the moments of truth in that particular business. Think about your own business. What are the various points of contact at which the customer passes judgement on your enterprise? How many opportunities do you have to score points?

To help your thinking process, visualize your organization as dealing with the customer in terms of a *cycle of service*, a repeatable sequence of events in which various people try to meet the customer's needs and expectations at each point. The cycle begins at the very first point of contact between the customer and your organization. It may be the instant at which the customer sees your advertisement, gets a call from your sales person, or initiates a telephone inquiry. Or it may be any other happening that starts the process of doing business. It ends, only temporarily, when *the customer* considers the service complete, and it begins anew when he or she decides to come back for more.

To help you discover the critical moments of truth in your dealings with your customers, try drawing a diagram of your particular service cycle. Divide the cycle into the smallest possible increments or episodes that make any sense conceptually. Then begin to identify the various moments of truth going on throughout the cycle. Try to associate particular moments of truth with specific stages of the customer's experience.

The service cycle will be unique for your particular business. It may vary from one customer to another, from one version of your service to another, and from one situation to another. At any moment, each customer who is doing business with you is somewhere in his or her uniquely personal cycle. Of course, customers don't usually think of their experiences consciously in terms of a cycle; they generally pay attention to whatever concrete needs they have at a particular moment. But it pays for you to think about this cycle in very specific stages, because it is the very substance of your business.

During a seminar with a group of health care administrators, we asked the participants to diagram the cycle of service that ensues when a patient is wheeled off for, and eventually brought back from, a series of medical tests. After several minutes of discussion about the place of various orderlies, nurses, doctors, and lab technicians in the cycle, the task was completed. As they sat admiring their handiwork, one of the administrators aloud—as much to himself as to the group—"My God! No one is in charge." His insight proved to be a valuable one that we have since seen revalidated in other professional service organizations. His explanation went approximately like this:

> Our hospital is organized and managed by professional speciality—by functions like nursing, housekeeping, security, pharmacy, and so on. As a result, no single person or group is really *accountable* for the overall success and quality of the patient's experience. The orderlies are accountable for a part of the experience, the nurses for another, the lab technicians for another, and so on. There are a lot of people accountable for a part of a service cycle, but no one has personal accountability for an *entire cycle of service.*

The generalization of this insight is that when you are organized along functional lines as opposed to product or service cycle lines, no one is responsible for ensuring that the cycle of service goes off effectively. In the abstract, of course, the chief executive of the organization is *accountable*, and everyone who comes in contact with the customer—in this example the patient—is *responsible*. But the simple fact remains that when no one is specifically accountable for the cycle of service, from beginning to end, the customer's experience with the organization is going unmanaged. When the customer's experience—the moments of truth—goes unmanaged, mediocrity prevails.

THREE FEATURES OUTSTANDING SERVICE ORGANIZATIONS HAVE IN COMMON

Three important characteristics differentiate outstanding service organizations from mediocre ones. We shall have a great deal to say about these factors in succeeding chapters, so we shall touch on them only briefly here.

A well-conceived strategy for service. The outstanding organizations have discovered, invented, or evolved a unifying idea about what they do. This service concept, or *service strategy* as we shall call it in later discussions, directs the attention of the people in the organization toward the real priorities of the customer. This guiding concept finds its way into all that people do. It becomes a rallying cry, a kind of gospel, and the nucleus of the message to be transmitted to the customer.

Customer-oriented frontline people. By some means the managers of such organizations have encouraged and helped the people who deliver the service to keep their attention fastened on the needs of the customer. The effective frontline person is able to maintain an "otherworldly" focus of attention by tuning in to the customer's current situation, frame of mind, and need. This leads to a level of responsiveness, attentiveness, and willingness to help that marks the service as superior in the customer's mind and makes him or her want to tell others about it and come back for more.

Customer-friendly systems. The delivery system that backs up the service people is truly designed for the convenience of the customer rather than the convenience of the organization. The physical facilities, policies, procedures, methods, and communication processes all say to the customer, "This apparatus is here to meet your needs."

These three factors—a clear service strategy, customer-oriented frontline people, and customer-friendly systems—are all relatively simple in concept and fairly easy to understand. Yet making them a reality is almost always a monumental task, especially in large organizations. Most of the remainder of this book deals with what we have found out about implementing service management by trying to actively manage these three critical factors.

THE TRIANGLE OF SERVICE

The obvious question facing us at this point in our discussion is, How shall we approach the *management of service?* What can the leaders of a service enterprise do that will directly or indirectly maximize the quality of the customer's experience at the many moments of truth? Is there now a perspective, some sort of framework, or a paradigm for thinking about the task of managing for outstanding service? Just as we need a model such as the cycle of service to understand the perspective of the customer, we need a company-oriented model to help managers think about what they need to do.

It is useful, we believe, to think of the company and the customer as intimately engaged in a triangular sort of relationship, like that shown in Figure 3–1. This *service triangle,* as we call it, represents the three elements of service strategy, people, and systems as more or less revolving around the customer in a creative interplay.

This triangle model is radically different from the standard organization charts we have traditionally used to think about business operations. It represents a *process* rather than a structure, and it forces us to include the customer in our conception of the business.

In the following chapters we will share what we know so far about each of these four key elements: customer, strategy, people, and systems. We'll devote a chapter to each element, but at this point let's make sure the big picture is reasonably clear.

If we are really going to practice what we preach about developing a customer-driven organization, it makes sense to start with the customer as our basis for defining the business. Of course, the company exists to serve the customer. That is supposedly understood. But let's go further and say that *the organization exists to serve the needs of the people who are serving the customer.* We must organize and manage for service, not just preach about it.

Once we have a clear conception of the motivational structure of the customer, we need to develop some kind of workable model

FIGURE 3–1 The Service Triangle

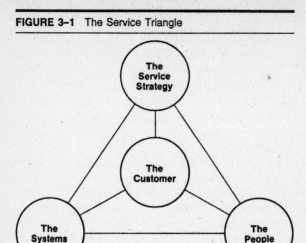

© 1984 Karl Albrecht

for service. We need to agree upon a basic business strategy that will serve to differentiate our company from our competitors in the mind and in the experience of our customers. In many cases, and probably most, it is a very challenging task to formulate a nontrivial philosophy of service that can really make a difference. Advertising slogans won't do it. The service strategy must mean something concrete and valuable to the customer, something he or she is willing to pay for.

Armed with an understanding of the customer's buying motivations and a concept for service that will position our company advantageously in the marketplace, we must then explore the interplay between the strategy, the people of our organization, and the systems that are available to them to get the job done.

It is instructive to some extent to take each of the parts of the service triangle more or less literally, and to explore some of the obvious interactions. Each of the lines in the diagram can represent an important dimension of impact. For example, the line connecting the customer and the service strategy can be taken to represent the critical importance of building the service strategy around the core needs and motives of the customer. This is no place for guesswork. We need to find out, if we don't really know, what goes on in our customer's mind when he or she thinks about our kind of service.

Conversely, the line that flows from the *service strategy* to the customer represents the process of communicating the strategy to our market. It is not nearly enough that we give good service, or that our service is uniquely better in some way; the customer has to know that fact for it to do us any good.

The line connecting the customer and the *people* of the organization explains itself. It is the crucial point of contact, the continuing interplay that accounts for most of the moments of truth. It is this interplay that presents the greatest opportunity for gain or loss, and for creative effort.

Another very interesting line on the service triangle figure connects the customer to the *systems* that presumably help to deliver the service. These systems can include abstract procedural systems as well as physical hardware. Many negative moments of truth in the business world arise because of system peculiarities and malfunctions. When the customer's interest is treated as an afterthought in the design of service delivery systems, the situation is virtually programmed for mediocrity and dissatisfaction.

Restaurant tables that are awkward or uncomfortable, cramped airline seats that jam people in like cattle, forms that don't make sense and are impossible to fill out, illogical or confusing building layouts, and administrative processes that burden the customer with tasks that could be handled by service employees all make it more difficult for the people to provide service effectively.

The three outer lines of the service triangle tell their own individual stories as well. For example, think about the interplay between the people and the systems. How often have you seen highly motivated people prevented from giving the quality of service they really wanted to give because of nonsensical administrative procedures, illogical task assignments, regressive work rules, or poor physical facilities? In situations like these, the service concept is nothing more than normal procedure.

Frontline people are usually much better prepared than their managers to find ways to improve the systems they use every day. The big question is, Do their managers realize that fact, and are they willing to invite the people to contribute what they know?

The line connecting the service strategy with the systems suggests that the design and deployment of the physical and administrative systems should follow logically from the definition of service strategy. This seems obvious, but given the inertial resistance to change found in most large organizations, it sometimes seems like a utopian precept.

And finally, what about the line that flows between the service strategy and the people? That line suggests that the people who deliver the service need to have the benefit of a clearly defined philosophy from management. Without some sense of focus, clarity, and priority, it is difficult for them to keep their attention on service quality. The moments of truth tend to deteriorate and regress to mediocrity.

We will explore the elements and implications of the service triangle in more depth in later chapters. At this point it is important to begin thinking about the interplay of the key components of service, and to think about getting them to work in harmony. Let's think about the companywide approach to service.

WHY HAVE A CUSTOMER SERVICE DEPARTMENT?

If a company that is supposed to be operating in a service industry has a department called the "customer service department," what are all the other departments supposed to be doing? Might it be that having a customer service department signals to the other people in the company that the customer is being properly looked after, and that they need not concern themselves with the matter? Shouldn't the entire organization be one large customer service department—at least figuratively speaking?

Think about some of the service organizations you have dealt with as a customer yourself. How do the people treat you when you have some kind of special need or peculiar problem? Do they take the initiative to help you solve it, or at least steer you far enough in the right direction? Or do they simply brush you off and mumble something about contacting "customer service"?

This type of behavior at the moments of truth is all too common, and it quickly establishes a process of regression to mediocrity. The prevailing point of view is, "I have my job to do. It's somebody else's job to take care of this customer's problem." This particular point bears some very careful thought. We can't say, of course, that a service employee must drop whatever he or she is doing at the moment and work the customer's problem through to completion. But the *perception* of service quality at the moment of truth revolves around the customer's sense of having been helped and appreciated. A skillful employee can do this in many creative ways and in the normal flow of work.

Jan Carlzon very often said to his frontline people, "SAS is *you.* In the mind of the customer, you are the company at that particular moment of truth. I want you to respond to the real need of the customer, and not use some standardized procedure for getting rid of him."

This is the same message stressed by Walt Disney when he created Disneyland, the "magic kingdom." Disneyland is all about fantasy. The customer is transported into a magical fairy tale, where all things are wonderful and all things are possible. Disney wanted every park employee to understand the meaning of this experience for the customers. He drilled the message into every single one of them: "You are Disneyland."

This point of view contends that everybody in the company who ever comes into contact with a customer, even accidentally, is potentially in a service role. The administrative person walking down the corridor of the hospital can smile and say hello to the patient who is coming in or going out. The maintenance person in the hotel can greet the guest in the elevator, and stop to give directions to the meeting rooms. The person in the gift shop at the airport can tell a passenger how to go about finding a lost item, or how to page someone.

In too many situations, at too many moments of truth, a "non-service" person turns a cold shoulder to a customer who needs help. This is the nature of the regression process. It takes many small moments of truth, handled in mediocre ways, to create a standard of mediocrity. The challenge to managers is to make sure that doesn't happen.

One of the most common symptoms of mediocrity in service is when the customer finds it necessary to run through an organizational maze to get his or her needs met. "That's not in this department," is an all too common answer. "You'll have to call House-keeping (or Patient Records, or Maintenance, or Residential Services, and so forth)." If you are forcing your customer to learn your organization to have a problem solved, you may want to reevaluate your corporate conception of service.

Before the break-up of AT&T, the old "Ma Bell" structure was famous for this customer runaround process. A person would call up the company with the need to have a telephone installed, or a service change, and end up dealing with three or more departments. In each case calling the department a second time got a completely different person, who had no prior knowledge of the order at all. Current indications are that dealing with the new AT&T will be at least as confusing as it was with the old telephone company for a fairly long time.

Banks often operate this way. Many branch banks are so compartmentalized and regimented in an attempt to eliminate all evidence of human judgement and initiative that very few people can steer a customer through the maze on their own. It is very common practice in dealing with banks to deal with people who know only one microscopic function, and who cannot offer a bit of help with any other.

None of these things occur out of malice. Service people don't get up in the morning and plan to abuse customers. What happens in so many of these situations is that nobody "owns" the responsibility for the solution to the customer's problem, and nobody sees the difference between carrying out job tasks and meeting customer needs. Service people can become so robotized in their actions that they greet any customer request with a standardized response, even if the response is only marginally effective.

It also helps to invite the "nonservice" people in the company to think of themselves as really being in service roles. Administrative people, accountants, computer specialists, engineers, contracts people, and staff people of various kinds tend to think of themselves as somehow removed from the din of battle. All too often they look upon service people as the ones who deal with *hoi polloi.* They are sometimes tempted to think of themselves as "above" the level of service roles. A strong and determined chief executive can disabuse them of this elitist viewpoint, and get them to thinking of service as a highly valued role.

When Robert Townsend took over as head of Avis Corporation and instituted its famous "We Try Harder" campaign, he decided that a bit of time behind the counter was therapeutic for every manager in the company. He issued a decree that even vice presidents were expected to do duty face-to-face with the customer.

He wanted all key people in the company to have first-hand knowledge of the needs and experiences of people who were using rental cars. He also wanted to dispel the connotation that the really important people were back at headquarters. The message, according to Townsend, was that the survival and prosperity of the company were in the hands of the people at the rental counters and in the maintenance shops, and that was where the action was.

Elitist attitudes and factional interests die hard in most organizations. Sometimes the accounting people act as if they think the organization exists so they can keep books on it. Some engineering people act as if the organization exists to support their intellectual hobbies. Some physicians act as if the hospital exists to cater to their overfed egos. It takes a very strong management to get the people in these various camps to see themselves as supporting the people and processes that deliver the quality of experience the customer considers important.

ORGANIZATIONAL SCHIZOPHRENIA: CONFLICTING PRIORITIES

If managing the moments of truth is the essence of service management, then the essential process in managing the moments of truth is building a *service-minded culture* in the organization. If the moments of truth go unmanaged and service quality regresses to mediocrity, there is usually a concomitant poverty of spirit among the people in the company overall. A "don't-give-a-damn" attitude creeps into the nooks and crannies of the collective psyche.

It becomes decidedly not "in" to act as if one cares about his or her job, or about performance or achievement, or about the satisfaction of the customer. Pride goes out the window, and the collective attention turns inward to the mundane and the trivial. Unless the leadership and inspiration are present, mediocrity tends to reinforce itself.

An even worse state of affairs, which exists in many large service organizations, is a sort of schizophrenic double standard. Top managers may talk about customer satisfaction, quality of service, and the like, and yet their day-to-day actions may be reinforcing something quite different—all too often, attention and obedience to themselves. This pattern of "asking for A and rewarding B" tends to create confusion, loss of motivation, and even cynicism among frontline people.

Outstanding service requires focused energy. Slogans will not do it. Posters will not do it. Inspirational memos will not do it. It will happen when the managers of organization step up to their responsibilities as leaders and articulate a concept of service which the people can find believable, feasible, worthwhile, and rewarding. The organizational climate must be ready and the management commitment must be present for service management to take root and thrive.

SERVICE MANAGEMENT: OLD WINE IN NEW BOTTLES?

In briefing hundreds of managers in a number of countries on the service management concept, and particularly in the United

States, we have frequently had to field the question, "So what's new? This is just the same old 'customer satisfaction' stuff that we've known about for years. Isn't service management just putting old wine in new bottles?"

Perhaps, but let's take a closer look at the bottles. In the United States we have long paid lip service to customer satisfaction. We have been fond of saying, "The customer is always right," "The customer comes first," and all the rest. And yet there has not been until now a clear-cut model for thinking about the *management* of service. American managers have tended to leave the matter of customer satisfaction to the customer service department. They typically assume that someone is taking proper care of the customer, unless the number of complaints begins to get too high. Then it becomes time for corrective action.

The service triangle provides a much needed conceptual framework for thinking about the quality of service, and for figuring out how to manage the moments of truth. Except for some special considerations about changing the culture of organizations, the rest of the theory is, admittedly, pretty much congruent with what is already known about customer service. But from our point of view as students of management, we believe the valuable contribution offered by the Scandinavian experience is the reconceptualization of service as a top-management concern.

4

The Customer: King or Peasant?

Understanding the perceptions of the customer is crucial to service success.
—*Karl Albrecht/Ron Zemke*

"The customer is king" is probably the most shopworn of all business slogans. It and catchphrases like it create an initial impression that a company is paying attention to the needs and interests of its customer. However, the real test is not in slogans but in the actual experience of the customer. Too often, the customer gets treated more like a peasant than a king or queen.

We confess to having become just a bit cynical about service slogans and catchphrases as a result of some years of working with organizations of various kinds. We have finally concluded that the correlation between service and slogans is essentially nil.

CUSTOMER PERCEPTIONS: WHAT HAVE YOU DONE FOR ME LATELY?

How you think you are perceived by the customer and how the customer actually perceives you can often be a great distance apart. Understanding the perceptions of the customer can be crucial to the success of a service-oriented business. It is not enough just to give good service; the customer must *perceive* the fact that he or she is getting good service. This raises some interesting considerations about the role of the customer and the role of the service organization as well as how each perceives the other.

First, we must acknowledge that the customer is not concerned with, and does not care about, the day-to-day problems inside the organization. Managers and employees can often forget this point, especially when they have to work with customers in less than ideal conditions. Scheduling difficulties, computer problems, inventory shortages, and labor disputes just don't register in the customer's mental scheme of things. The customer's only real concern in the situation is with getting his or her own very specific needs met.

Customers are usually not interested in whether you are "trying hard." They only want solutions to their own problems. Service employees too often get caught up in the peculiar problems of their organization and lose touch with this simple but critical fact. The customer is self-centered. There is no particular reason to believe that things should be otherwise.

Loyalty is another concept that is often discussed in service-oriented organizations. "Product loyalty" and "customer loyalty" are phrases that advertising and marketing people use when discussing sales leads and demographic surveys. The fact of the matter is that there is no such thing as customer loyalty, at least in the sense that many customer/product-oriented people conceive it to exist.

The three key facts about customer loyalty are that it is circumstantial, it is fragile, and it is fleeting. Loyalty begins to fade as the level of service declines below expectations. The customer wants and expects the service to be at a suitable level all of the time. When the level of service no longer meets his or her expectations, the customer exercises other options, if they are available, and looks for satisfaction. This is not to say that the concept of customer loyalty is completely invalid, only that it must be based on a continuously satisfying level of service.

A good example of a marriage between loyalty and service can be seen at the famous Sears Restaurant in San Francisco. The owner, Al Boyajian, has been operating the business five days a week for 32 years. The restaurant serves breakfast and lunch and averages between 800 and 900 checks a day. It often takes up to 45 minutes to gain a seat inside, but longtime patrons feel the wait is well worth it for a variety of reasons. The main reason is Boyajian's nearly compulsive attention to quality and service. His is a hands-on approach to the business of providing high-quality service and the best food he can supply.

Boyajian is constantly in touch with his customers and keeps asking for their suggestions about the "little" things. He believes that "my customers should be treated like guests in my own home." His customers are intensely loyal to *him* because that is the same impression he conveys to them.

VISIBLE SERVICES AND INVISIBLE SERVICES

It is instructive to think about service in two distinct ways: visible service and invisible service. When service is highly visible—as is the case in the San Francisco restaurant—it has a different impact on the customer than when it is relatively invisible. Some services come to us in such a way that we have little cause to stop and think about them. The services supplied by gas and electric companies are an example of invisible service. Theirs is a relatively "invisible" service in that we rarely stop to wonder how or why our lights come on each time we flip the switch.

By the same token, the power company becomes highly "visible" on at least two distinct occasions: when we get our monthly bill, and when we flip the light switch and the lights *do not* come on. At this point our perceptions about the quality of service the company provides can change radically. Few people can open their utility bill without making some mental or vocal comment about the high cost of providing us with lights and power.

This perception, of course, is not entirely fair to the power companies because it is clear that most of them give fast and reliable service to their customers, especially in times of crisis. Most customer surveys show that people in the United States feel basically satisfied with the quality and reliability of their gas and electric services. While the power companies can do little to stop the rising cost of energy bills, they can counterbalance this built-in negative image by providing highly reliable service whenever they can.

Much of the utility companies' negative public image as service organizations comes from being a favorite target for the media, particularly the newspapers. When a utility company attempts to raise its rates, it takes a whipping in the newspapers at least four times. One hit comes when the request is formally introduced to the Public Utilities Commission, again during the rate-increase hearing, again when the commission approves the increase, and then a final time when the increase goes into effect. This protracted process of rate reviews and decision making gives the local papers a reliable news issue. The semiconscious impression in the mind of the customer is, "Those crooks are raising the rates every time I turn around!"

While the customer gives little thought to "invisible" services such as those on the other side of the light switch, there are some services he or she can't help thinking about. Consider for example, a trip to the dentist's office or flying in a commercial airplane. The customer is continuously aware of the service and highly conscious of "getting his money's worth" during each of these experiences.

The trip to the dentist is typically a threatening experience for most people, and they tend to watch everything done by the doctor or the office staff very critically. This also happens to some extent in airline travel. Unless a person travels extensively in connection with work, a trip on a commercial airline can be an exciting and even stressful event. Airline travel is fairly expensive, and people want to feel they're getting high-quality service for their dollar. Any deviation from this expectation can leave the customer with a negative perception about the entire experience.

THE PRICE OF IGNORANCE ABOUT THE CUSTOMER'S MOTIVATIONS

The directors of an art museum in a large midwestern city wanted to attract more visitors to the museum. They decided to survey the people who came into the museum on a certain day, to find out more about their interests. The museum employees handed out survey cards to the visitors as they entered the museum. The people filled out the cards and dropped them into a box as they left the building.

Later, staff members analyzed the results. One of the key questions on the survey was, "Why did you come into the museum today?" The most frequently given answer was, "Because it was raining outside." The second most popular answer was, "To use the bathroom." Imagine the state of mind of the museum's operators in the face of this kind of feedback from their "customers." Strictly speaking, an art museum has customers just like any other service establishment. If people did not come in to look at the art, the museum would not be able to operate. This is a prime example of the business operator knowing too little about the motivations of the customer.

When the customer comes into contact with a service organization he or she sees the entire picture, not just one element of it. We have previously referred to this totality of experience and perception as the cycle of service. To use a commercial airline as an example, the cycle of service starts when the customer calls to book a reservation for a particular flight. It continues as the customer goes to the airport, buys the ticket, checks luggage at the flight counter, boards the plane, eats a meal or watches a movie while in flight, lands at a specific city, and carries out his or her business until it is time for the return trip home. The process is repeated in reverse, and the cycle is complete when both customer and luggage are safe at home.

At each point of this cycle, the customer comes into contact with one specific part of the organization. The perceptions of the customer can be altered or influenced by any person or factor encountered along the way.

From this standpoint we can see that the customer has a certain distinctive paradigm or conceptual frame of reference in mind, while the various airline employees have their own individual paradigms. Each employee has a grip on only "one leg of the elephant," so to speak, being well versed in his or her own specific job tasks, but typically unfamiliar with the tasks or responsibilities of other employees.

Consider the following episode: a customer is walking through the airport terminal and does not know where to find the boarding gate for the particular airline he or she wishes to take. The customer may ask for directions from a baggage handler who happens to be walking by. Now even though the baggage handler may be an employee of that same airline, it just so happens that he is on his lunch break. One answer to the customer's question could be for the handler to grunt and point vaguely off into one direction as he forces a sandwich into his mouth.

What, if any, positive outcomes could arise from this customer-employee encounter? Another, more positive answer would be if the baggage handler stopped and said, "Oh yes, sir (or ma'am), the gate you are looking for is down that hall and to your right." Each of the two possible replies takes the same amount of time, but the latter leaves a much more favorable impression with the customer in the long run.

In this example we can see that the baggage handler may not work at the boarding gate and may be unfamiliar with the employees or the procedures there. However, if he has any kind of corporate knowledge—which comes from proper customer service training, he will politely give the customer, who indirectly pays his salary, enthusiastic help and service.

Again, the customer probably doesn't notice that it is the baggage handler's lunch break. He or she merely wants to get to the boarding gate to catch the plane. This is the customer's primary motivation at that particular place and time, and nothing else matters very much. Brief encounters like this make or break every phase of the airline's existence.

All the airline's efforts at marketing, advertising, and goodwill can be either greatly enhanced or ruined by an appropriate or rude response by a single employee. This is just one example of the need for service orientation on the part of *all* employees, not just those whose jobs are defined as public contact-oriented.

Ignorance about customer motivations continue to plague many service organizations. One booming market—the personal computer industry—has seen only limited growth after its early rise in popularity and productivity. An important reason for this slowed growth is the lack of acceptance of the computer by the "pragmatist" population, the people who still see the process of learning to deal with computers as too punishing for their temperament.

These pragmatists represent the third stage of a five-stage technology diffusion process recognized by sociologists:

1. Experimenters—people who like to toy with almost any new gadget, experience, or style.
2. Early adopters—people who like to put new things to practical use.
3. Pragmatists—the majority who try a new technology only after it's proven and "here to stay."
4. Late adopters—people who accept it when forced to.
5. Resisters—people who actively reject it.

According to this theory, experimenters and early adopters have been the majority of computer buyers up until now. They are people with a strong technical orientation who enthusiastically greet and try a new technology. Unfortunately, there appears to be a distinct gap developing between the first two types of people and the third.

Pragmatists seem to be significantly different from experimenters and early adopters. There is increasing evidence that the pragmatists are not rushing into computers as many industry people thought and hoped that they would. The mental temperaments of pragmatists are different, their values are different, their technical orientations are different, and their personal needs are very different.

Many companies that make computers, publish software, and offer books on the subject can't quite seem to connect with the needs and motivations of this element of the market. Advertisements still geared to the highly technical person reveal an expectation on the part of the makers of computers that somehow there won't be a gap between the stages of adoption.

The computer manufacturers seem to be hoping that the next wave of buyers will commit their money in the same ways and for the same reasons as the people from the first two waves. The assumption appears to be that everyone will learn to love the computer in time, and that no special concessions will have to be made to win the commitment of the remainder of the population.

The diffusion theory suggests that a distinct gap will indeed develop, based on the radically different technical orientations of the people in the various stages. As the number of experimenters and early adopters who don't already have computers grows smaller, the manufacturers are finding it harder to sell their products into this diminishing market segment.

Just as most computer and software developers have not yet learned how to create products that interest the pragmatists, most advertising companies have not learned how to present their ads to this segment of the market. Computer and software ads for the most part focus on technical characteristics, sophisticated features, and other factors that only interest the highly technical buyer. These ads are rarely written in plain English, and this only serves to hurt the advertisers and the companies they promote.

HOW CUSTOMERS FALL IN AND OUT OF LOVE

Today's fad may be tomorrow's antique. A reliable, profitable line of business can eventually fade into obscurity if times change and customer needs or interests change. Very few of the businesses existing today existed 50 years ago in anything like their present form. Conversely, many profitable businesses of yesteryear found it necessary to change or die.

The history of organizations as adaptive entities is anything but impressive. It is all too common for a company to experience a radical change in the structure of its industry, and yet utterly fail to mobilize its resources to cope with the change. It seems to be exceedingly difficult to redeploy the technology, resources, and attitudes of a large organization in any radical way. We can learn a great deal about adapting to changing customer needs by studying the history of organizations that have adapted poorly, as well as those that have adapted well.

Let's look at churches for a moment. Churches as a group have a real marketing problem, as shown by the fact that attendance and revenues have steadily declined for years. The American churches used to provide spiritual guidance as well as serve as meeting places and centers of influence for people in small townships. In the past the churches were perhaps the only sources of social contact in rural communities. But people in today's "mobi-centric" society find this contact quite readily in their jobs, social groups, and neighborhoods. Most churches have failed to adapt their "products" to the changing environment of their "customers."

Another noteworthy case of getting out of touch with the customer's needs can be seen in the decline of the Boy Scouts. For many years the Boy Scouts carried on a patriotic American tradition that helped boys become responsible young men. The values and ideals taught by this historical service organization have contributed to the lives of many famous men. Presidents, athletes, and actors attributed many personal benefits to their membership in the Boy Scouts.

But what of today's Scouts? Membership has fallen dramatically for the simple reason that young boys have so many other options in their lives. Television, for one, is far more prevalent than it was thirty years ago when the Scouts were popular. Today young boys have their own set of values that are influenced by other ideas that have replaced scouting. When a boy reaches the age where scouting might appeal to him, he may have already decided that he would rather spend his time at home in front of the TV.

Scouting has failed to make the transition into the modern era. The movement needs a more powerful personal appeal to recruit young boys and to promote the worthy values that scouting provides. Its recruiting efforts stagnated and failed to meet the boys' needs. Scouting administrators are now hard at work rethinking what they can and should offer to our youth. Without first understanding the motivations and needs of their "customers," it is impossible for the administrators to offer appealing options.

Service companies sometimes fail to meet changing needs even when they are ideally positioned to lead the way. Two industries, in particular, fell victim to the technological "leapfrog" effect that seems to characterize innovation in many fields. Both the hotel industry and the railroad industry missed significant opportunities to expand and develop new customer-service concepts in new industries. The hotels and railroads failed to capitalize on the changing needs of their customers. They did not see that the American middle class was changing, and that it was growing and becoming more mobile.

The hotel industry was always a thriving business that catered to the travel needs of the upper and middle classes. However, as America expanded and our transportation capabilities grew, we discovered that we needed inexpensive places to stay that could save us time and money. The American travel market was ripe for clean, inexpensive rooms located near airports and interstate highways.

Presumably the hotel industry should have led the way in creating the motel industry. Hotel executives had the knowledge and expertise required to serve the needs of the American traveler. It would have seemed only logical that they would have put money and effort into developing the motel industry as a logical extension of their own businesses. But in fact the motels arose as almost a separate industry altogether. The Hiltons, Marriotts, and Sheratons did not pioneer low-cost, convenient lodging. That innovation required an entirely new set of players.

The railroad industry was a real success story from its origins until the late 1940s. Train travel was popular, low-priced, and relatively efficient. Many people rode the trains and many companies used their services to haul freight throughout the nation. During its heyday the train was more popular than the automobile for service and dependability on long trips. However, the onset of the commercial airline industry and the railroad companies' failure to utilize their knowledge of mass transportation resulted in the decline of the railroad industry as a whole.

Again, the railroad industry should have logically led the way in developing the new airline industry. Railroad executives were the transportation industry's leaders and experts. Their knowledge should have contributed to and effectively developed the airplane as an option for travel technology. Who could better capitalize on the new passenger and freight-moving industry than the current leaders in the transportation field? However, the airline companies came along with an aggressive new leadership and rapidly became popular with the travel and freight customer.

Customers found that air travel was cheaper, faster, and more efficient. Freight companies found that the airlines could get products to their destinations with a minimum of delay. Meanwhile, the railroad companies had neglected their recapitalization responsibilities, and much of the rolling stock became outdated and often unsafe. Freight schedules were mismanaged, causing long delays in service.

As the years passed, the airline companies took bold steps to capitalize on the increase in business travel by providing frequent service runs along short metropolitan corridors as well as coast-to-coast trips. Airline companies clinched their superiority over the railroads by applying computer technology to flight scheduling and ticket sales, and by staging successive upgrades of aircraft equipment introduced by the major manufacturers.

Railroad executives failed in two major areas. First, they did not anticipate the impact of the commercial airliner on their own business; as a result, they did not contribute their expertise to this new form of transportation. Second, they failed to upgrade their technology, services, and equipment to match their customers' changing demands. This rigidity and inability to adapt contributed heavily to the decline in popularity and use of the railroads.

One firm that did see change coming and met it with an effective business strategy was Sears, Roebuck & Co. Sears became the largest retail company in the world by getting its goods to its customers. At the turn of the century, the Sears management decided to focus on farmers and people in rural communities as their prime customers. The people at Sears realized that they would have to develop an effective distribution channel since Americans were spread all over the country and were relatively immobile.

Sears settled on the mail-order approach, thus opening up an important economic trend that lasted for many years. Retail stores in the cities offered a reliable source of business as well, but the main focus for Sears was on the rural dwellers who then made up over 80 percent of the population. The small purchases of individual farmers added up to an enormous buying power.

In the 20s and 30s, however, the automobile made the American people more mobile, and many of them migrated to the cities to take industrial jobs. As the American middle class emerged with new buying patterns, the Sears management adapted to the demographic changes and decided on a new sales thrust. They elected to shift the focus of their operation to retail stores. This meant a sweeping change in the structure and operation of the entire company. Today farmers make up less than 5 percent of the American population. Since Sears now operates a large and successful chain of retail stores in our heavily urban society, we can see that the company has made some very strategic customer-service maneuvers.

THE IMPORTANCE OF MARKET RESEARCH

Market research plays a crucial role in enabling an organization to change and develop with its customers. In a nutshell market research tells the service company how it is perceived by its customers and what its possibilities may be. Some companies invest heavily in market research, while others invest surprisingly little. There is no correct level of investment, of course, but it makes sense to gather as much information as is needed to be sure we understand the motivational structure of the customer, how that customer perceives our organization, and what our possibilities are for improving our stance.

Effective market research usually deals with two kinds of information: *demographic* and *psychographic*. Demographic information is concerned with the general human characteristics that serve to identify specific segments of the customer population. Demographics typically include age, gender, education, income bracket, family size, and type of housing. This kind of information gives a statistical overview of the customer population.

Psychographic information is concerned with attitudes, preferences, beliefs, value systems, social habits, and expectations. Psychographic information is usually more difficult and costly to gather than demographic information. Demographics are often available from public sources, but psychographics are in the minds of people. Typically, the only way to get this kind of attitudinal information is to go out and ask for it.

As we have emphasized in previous discussions, the customer carries around in his or her head a kind of invisible report card, which forms the basis of a grading system to which the service organization is subjected. Frequently the report card is an unconscious one. Most people, in their roles as customers, react to specific incidents but do not necessarily generalize. If you ask people why they like a particular bank or hotel or airline more than another, they will probably come up with good reasons. But they usually don't go around giving conscious grades to service companies in any comprehensive way.

There is often a great deal of assuming and guessing going on in service organizations about the customer's attitudes and habits. It is common for those who run service organizations to form their views of the customers through long years of experience but with little actual data. Each manager has a theory about what is important to the customer, but in relatively few cases is this theory actually grounded in reasonably sophisticated research.

In the words of the noted researcher Sherlock Holmes, "It is a capital mistake to theorise before one has data." An earlier chapter of this book has pointed out the importance of understanding the customer's buying motivations. What does the buyer expect from a service like the one we provide? What factors make a difference in his or her mind? What leads the buyer to patronize our service instead of all the other options available? In working with service organizations, we often find that managers have only the vaguest notions about what really counts in the mind of the customer.

Here is a small but telling example, shared by a trainer in the hotel industry who attended one of our service management workshops. She had been conducting a seminar of her own with the various managers and supervisors in her hotel. The activity focused extensively on the quality of customer service. As the time approached for the coffee break, someone in the group asked, "What are the moments of truth involved in such a simple thing as a coffee break? What factors are important in a good break?" This led to a quick survey of the group to find out what they as individuals considered important in a coffee break.

Some time later the trainer conducted a little outside research. She asked the server who tended the coffee table what he thought made for a good coffee break. She also requested the opinions of the food and beverage manager and the manager of the hotel. The server, the food and beverage manager, and the hotel manager all agreed that the coffee should be of the highest quality, well-brewed, and served in attractive china. It should be served from a polished, elegant coffee urn on a clean, attractively arranged table.

None of the people in the workshop mentioned any of these factors in their survey. They wanted to get through the line at the coffee service quickly without having to mill around in a mob scene trying to get a cup of coffee or tea. They also wanted the coffee service area to be located close to the restrooms and telephones, a factor that none of the planners had considered. It turned out that the participants thought of the coffee in the overall context of a total break that would take care of a variety of needs. None of them even mentioned the quality or flavor of the coffee.

"I wonder," mused our hotel trainer, "how often we may be trying to appeal to our customers with things they really don't care about?"

It is risky to assume that we know what people want and will pay for. Managers who have had little experience in gathering or analyzing psychographic information tend to give little thought to the process. Many of them rely on the "obvious facts" they know about their customers. But as we have seen in the example of the coffee break, what we think is obvious may not even be true. To quote Sherlock Holmes again, "There is nothing so deceptive as an obvious fact."

The kinds of market information we need to gather depend largely on the kinds of service we are offering and the kinds of strategic options we are considering. For example, if we are a hospital that would like to expand into the field of health and wellness, we need to anticipate how our present customers might respond to such a move. Would they see us as a plausible supplier of those needs? What expectations do they have of achieving them? What kinds of experience do they picture when they think of physical fitness? What sort of facility would they expect? What sort of marketing message would make sense to them?

If we are a specialty magazine publishing firm that would like to publish a line of books related to the same field, we would want to know if our readers might see us as a logical source for such books. Would we be competing with publishers who advertise with us? Do we have credibility that we can bank on? Will our endorsement of a particular book add strength to its sales? How well do we understand our readers' needs for books? A magazine is one thing; books may represent a totally different relationship with our customers.

If we are considering trying to change the image of our product or service, how well do we understand the image that our customers currently have of it? Advertising guru David Ogilvy likes to tell the story of his early experience with household products, particularly the bath soap Dove. His advertising strategy was to declare that this new product was not really a soap, but something different, new, and superior to ordinary soap. His print media campaign featured the slogan, "Dove makes soap obsolete." He was pleased with his early efforts until a readership study of the ad revealed that 40 percent of the people reading the ad did not know what the word *obsolete* meant. It can be a grave error to underestimate the difficulty, time, and resources involved in communicating an abstract concept or benefit to a market, as many personal computer and software companies are finding out, for instance.

Learning what the customer thinks is important and can present a real challenge. There is an art to knowing what information to look for and how to ask the right questions to find it out. Much of what passes for market research is really opinion data based on preformatted questions. If you ask people attending a concert at intermission time how they like the music, the seats, and the refreshments, they will give you their evaluations. But if you forget to ask them how they came to the concert hall, you will probably never discover that many of them find the neighborhood threatening and often don't come to that hall because they are apprehensive about leaving their cars parked in an undesirable area.

Good market research involves a skillful form of exploration that enables us to discover important information. This is true even if we don't know exactly what questions to ask.

IMAGE AS A MANAGED PERCEPTION

Finally, we offer some thoughts about the service image. What are some of the factors that come to your mind when you hear the word *image*? These might include terms like goodwill, credibility, honesty, ethics, reputation, trust, a sense of permanence, consistency, quality, and integrity. These are some of the images a company can have. But what is an image?

A practical definition of the term *image* from the standpoint of business strategy is "a managed perception on the part of the customer of the way the company does business." How do we want our customers to perceive us? What kind of an image do we want to *earn* by the way we conduct our affairs?

Understanding how a company's image is created is critical to the process of building one. The moments of truth concept reminds us that our image improves or deteriorates moment to moment and day by day as a result of the sum total of our customer's experiences in dealing with us. We manage the customer's perception—our image—by managing the moments of truth.

It is a curious fact that the three biggest service bargains in American society all come from institutions that have basically negative service images. These are the gas and electric service, the telephone system, and the mail system. Think about the cost of mailing a letter, for instance, in terms of the number of minutes you would need to work at your job in order to earn enough to pay for it. The equivalent cost is trivial. Consider your "labor cost" for a telephone call, even at long distance rates. When it comes to your home heating bill, consider what you would have to do on your own to gather and burn enough fuel to give yourself the same comfort level you get by twisting the knob on your thermostat.

While it is fair to say that these three service organizations are not always brilliantly managed, they do provide valuable services for the prices we pay. Yet it is ironic that most customers are singularly unimpressed with these three institutions, which might have image problems even if they always gave effective service, were represented by well-qualified frontline people, and had customer-friendly systems. The one aspect of the service triangle all of these organizations seem to neglect is the service strategy. They do not do an adequate job of *communicating* their services to their customers. Most of them take a relatively passive role, based on the assumption that good service will earn them high marks.

This assumption is clearly faulty. To improve their images, these institutions need to project a clearer, more believable message to the public. They need to show their customers what value is received for the money they pay. In other words these organizations ought to develop service strategies that emphasize customer awareness of their strong points.

Let's return now to the concept of the service triangle (see Figure 3–1). When we can find the elements of (1), a meaningful service strategy (2), customer-oriented frontline people and (3), customer-friendly systems working in self-reinforcing interplay, we are doing what is necessary to earn a positive image. We are creating such an image indirectly by managing the customer's experience. We are reinforcing his or her perception of our organization by making things come out right at the moments of truth.

5

Finding the Service Strategy

> One of the most important things an organization can do is determine exactly what business it is in.
> —*Peter Drucker*

Proceeding with our step-by-step exploration of the service triangle, we come to the *service strategy*. Now that we've clarified the role of the customer's viewpoint and motivational structure, we need to think through the options available in "positioning" the service organization in the marketplace.

Management theorist Peter Drucker suggests that one of the most important things an organization can do is to determine exactly what business it is in. That is especially true of service organizations. What precisely their goal is may often not be clear because no tangible product comes rolling off of the assembly line. All who deal with the design and delivery of a service should have the same concept of that service and its purposes for the consumer. This is true whether the service is the primary product or simply a "bundled" or secondary attribute of the product.

In this chapter we'll suggest answers to the most challenging questions facing every service organization that needs to make the quality of its service a top priority:

1. What is a service strategy?
2. Why should we have a formal service strategy?
3. When is it necessary to rethink such a strategy?
4. What are the ingredients of an effective service strategy? (What elements does it contain?)
5. What does a typical service strategy look like? (What does it say?)

Defining or revising the service strategy is often a challenging and creative task. In some cases good market research will clearly indicate a way to position the organization in the customer's mind. In other cases it might be necessary to wrestle with some complex questions and issues and to apply a great deal of executive judgement. In a later chapter we'll suggest some management methods for developing a service strategy. Here we'll simply talk about the thought processes behind an effective service strategy.

WHAT IS A SERVICE STRATEGY?

While there is no one approved answer to the first question, "What is a service strategy?" here is a workable definition:

> A service strategy is a distinctive formula for delivering service; such a strategy is keyed to a well-chosen benefit premise that is valuable to the customer and that establishes an effective competitive position.

Vision plays an important role in developing a service strategy. Vision is the ability to "see the forest through the trees." Seeing the forest means realizing what is in the marketplace around your organization, analyzing your position in that marketplace, and developing a clear concept of the position you want to occupy. This is a sophisticated, entrepreneurial thought process that demands judgement, creativity, and the ability to think on a global level.

Many organizations do what they do because that is what they were doing last year, the year before, and the year before that. The great flywheel of habit keeps a lot of companies on the same straight path long after it has become clear that they will face tougher times unless they learn to adapt. It takes a great deal of energy, determination, and intellectual courage to question the basic purposes of your business. Yet this is exactly what more and more executives are having to do as the structure of American industry continues to shift, as old markets dry up, and as new markets develop.

The ability to define and articulate a vision of service is becoming more and more needed in more and more industries. The caretaker executive, the action-oriented leader who likes to "ride to the sound of the guns," and the tradition-bound executive specialist all face a greater risk of becoming obsolete or of making their organizations obsolete. More and more the premium will be on setting the strategic direction of a company in terms of a market-oriented service strategy.

Another way of defining service strategy is to describe it as an *organizing principle* that allows people in a service enterprise to channel their efforts toward benefit-oriented services that make a significant difference in the eyes of the customer. This principle can guide everyone from top management on down to line and staff employees. The principle must make a statement that says, "This is what we are, this is what we do, and this is what we believe in." Adherence to this principle helps the company make service decisions within its realm of concern.

Still another variation on the definition of a service strategy is the following: a *concept that describes the value to be offered.* This point of view focuses on the nature of the customer's experience with the service. It revolves around the notion that value in the eyes of the customer is what counts, not necessarily value in the eyes of the company's marketing or advertising people.

If this concept is sufficiently definitive and benefit-oriented, it can serve effectively as the basis of an advertising campaign, that is, as a public statement announcing to customers the company's desire to provide good products and service. It can also become a corporate statement emphasizing to every employee the importance of providing high-quality customer service and an explanation of exactly what quality service means.

WHY HAVE A SERVICE STRATEGY?

What good does it do to announce a service strategy? Is it necessary to come up with a carefully phrased statement of some sort, and what do you do with it once you have it?

First, an effective service strategy "positions" your service in the marketplace. It gives you a simplified way to present your message—in a form that makes sense, has significance, and connects to a known buying need or motivational factor. The concept of positioning a service or a service organization in the marketplace, in the same sense as one positions a physical product, is rather new to the thinking of executives In Marketing 101 every business student hears about the concept of product positioning as an essential step in the development of market strategy. A Porsche occupies a different position—i.e., it appeals to a different set of values and preferences—than a Mercedes or a Honda. Porsche buyers may be similar to other car buyers in some ways, but when it comes to the choice of a car, they want certain specific things and are willing to pay for them.

We can position a physical product distinctively even if it is quite similar to other products in its category. For example, in selling toothpaste we can present an appeal based on good health ("it prevents tooth decay") or an appeal based on sex appeal ("it makes your teeth whiter, your smile brighter"). Each of these different positioning approaches suggests a different approach to the message of the advertisement. Similarly, we have options for positioning a service in terms of personal benefits ("fly in comfort and style") or utilitarian benefits ("we get you there on time").

Because corporations have not typically thought of service as a managed proposition, or as a skillfully marketed proposition, the concept of positioning has not carried over easily into service advertising. You can quickly identify service organizations that do not have a clear sense of their market positioning: their advertisements don't say anything. When the marketing and advertising people don't know what the real battle cry is, they have no choice but to resort to puffy, low-content messages.

For example, although many hotel chains invest heavily in full-page four-color ads in airline magazines and business periodicals, many of their ads look vaguely alike. There may be a shot of a hotel lobby, a room, a pretty young desk clerk, or a "happy people" shot that is, a scene of rich, powerful, expensively dressed people having dinner in the hotel's restaurant or a drink in the lounge. You could easily interchange photographs, captions, and corporate logos, and it would make little or no difference.

Many hotels also have trouble positioning their meeting and conference services, which can be very profitable. A typical commercial brochure advertising hotel meeting facilities has lavish photographs of the golf course, swimming pool, and restaurant, and maybe an occasional shot of an empty conference room. Catering people are often expert at putting customers up for the night and feeding them, but they often don't seem to have even the foggiest idea of what business people actually do during their meetings.

At an executive retreat, for instance, the priority is on business, not golf. The senior management group may spend two or three full days locked up in a conference room, wrestling with the strategic issues of the business. They like the idea of having recreational facilities available, but they choose the hotel largely on its ability to support their business activities. It would seem to make more sense to promote the personalized support services that can make things go smoothly during a meeting.

Banks have also had a difficult time figuring out how to make themselves recognizable to customers. Their radio spots and print ads tend to be pathetically "vanilla" in content. Many resort to radio jingles in the hope of getting their names, at least, to sink into the minds of listeners. Yet after years of this kind of advertising, the man (or woman) on the street still thinks that banks are just banks.

Banks in California seem to have a penchant for pictures of golf courses in their advertisements. Apparently the abstract message is: "If you put your money in our bank, it will grow, you'll become wealthy, and you'll have plenty of time to play golf." The fact that relatively few people play golf—combined with the rather diffuse message of the commercial—means that the only part of the ad that communicates is the part giving the bank's name. If it's a billboard ad, the typical five-second exposure means that even the name probably won't get across.

When your company has a clearly defined service strategy which is based on value to your customer, the advertising people can use their most creative and effective techniques to communicate that message to the marketplace.

The second advantage of a clearly stated service strategy is that it provides a unifying direction for the organization. It lets managers at all levels know what the business is all about, what the key operational priorities are, and what they should be trying to accomplish.

Third, it lets service at the front line know what management expects of them and what is important in the organization. A distinct service strategy that has been well explained to all employees establishes the company belief that "service to the customer is the most important criterion to our company's success." It tells them how they will know that kind of service when they see it.

WHEN IS IT NECESSARY TO RETHINK THE SERVICE STRATEGY?

Service organizations usually rethink their basic service strategies for two reasons: (1) in order to anticipate changes in the market; or (2) in response to a crisis caused when they become dangerously out of touch with the market. Unfortunately, the latter case is much more common.

The first situation usually occurs when the executives of a company systematically and regularly evaluate the company's relationship to its public. This may take the form of an annual executive retreat, a strategy session, or a planning review. Such executives come together to review their financial performance, market data, and important trends in the business.

Anticipating changes in the needs or motivations of the customer is the key to realigning your company's service strategy. This is coupled with the concept of "forward vision" that was discussed previously in this chapter. Effective service organizations constantly watch the marketplace for signals that may foreshadow important changes in the consumer's needs, preferences, or buying motivations. The time to rethink the service strategy of your company is before these trends get into full swing, not afterward when it may be too late to slow the customer exodus to other companies, services, or products.

Systematic market research provides answers to corporate questions concerning current consumer behavior. But in order to develop a sound service strategy, you need more than just market research. Strategic thinking, planning, strength analysis, and opportunity mapping are organizational approaches that analyze what is happening in the marketplace.

The second, and unfortunately all too common, occasion for rethinking the service strategy occurs when an organization is shocked into reacting to a crisis. A severe drop in sales or a significant loss in its market share comes to the attention of the senior management group. At this point, however, it may not be easy to figure out what steps you should take to remedy the situation.

In such cases a number of confusion factors may make it difficult to recognize the need to rethink your service strategy. Executives may lose valuable months, or even years, debating what they should do. Without reliable market research information and a thorough service audit, the executives may not realize that they have lost touch with the real driving factors of customer motivation. The difference between these two modes of adaptation is the difference between "proactive" and "reactive" executive styles. In the first example your company takes steps to rethink its service strategy before the marketplace changes. It is taking a proactive position by anticipating new customer needs as the changes take place. In the second example your firm reacts to the changing marketplace by taking steps to change its services and products in order to keep your customers from moving to new suppliers. Unfortunately, the trends may be so strongly under way by the time your organization starts to adapt that it can take a painfully long period of time to win your customers back.

WHAT ARE THE INGREDIENTS OF A SERVICE STRATEGY?

An effective service strategy brings three important concepts into play: market research, the business mission, and the driving values of the organization. By combining these three fundamental thought processes, it is possible to evolve a meaningful approach to customer needs and expectations that will make a difference in the marketplace.

Reliable market research and the proper analysis of its findings is one of your first points of departure in arriving at a good service strategy. Effective service companies utilize all available information to help in strategic service planning. They place a high value on continuous investigation of their environments.

Another important element is a statement of the mission of your organization. What are we in business to do? This mission statement can take the form of a specific business charter or company policy statement that outlines the unique business proposition of the organization. It may be brief and pithy, or it may be extensive. This is largely a matter of personal preference among the company executives. In any case the mission statement should spell out your target market, the type of service offered to that market, and the distinctive means of approaching that market which your company will use.

The third fundamental element of an effective service strategy is a set of clearly stated and well-publicized corporate principles, which are the beliefs and values of your organization. The creation of a sound set of corporate principles, especially principles about service, leads to a more creative approach to the business of providing service. This can often help to establish the competitive edge a company may need to win out over less service-oriented competition.

If any of these three elements is missing, it makes good sense for top management to get them in place. Trying to develop a service strategy without a clear understanding of the realities of the marketplace, the real mission of the organization, or the driving values that top management wants to advocate can be a frustrating and unproductive experience.

In our work with organizations, we have often found that clarifying the corporate mission statement and getting agreement on the primary principles to be taught throughout the organization have contributed immensely to a better understanding of the business and a clearer sense of service priorities.

WHAT DOES A GOOD SERVICE STRATEGY LOOK LIKE?

We will try to answer the fifth and final question—"What does a typical service strategy look like?"—with a series of case vignettes, analyzing the apparent strategies of effective service-aware companies. These companies offer a diverse range of products and services, but you can see recurring themes throughout each corporate operation. They all have clearly defined service strategies to which they adhere. While the top management teams of the respective companies may have differing corporate philosophies and goals, they agree that customer service is the key to their success. Let's look at some typical organizations that have developed, implemented, and followed effective service strategies.

McDonald's restaurants. We are all familiar with this long-running, worldwide restaurant franchise system. For most of its 30 years, McDonald's has been the industry leader in the highly competitive fast-food marketplace. The company leads by example and its competitors try to follow its latest moves. The organization is a success because each store follows well-designed restaurant management principles.

The company spends a great deal of time in testing new food products before introducing them and in improving the already efficient customer-delivery systems. MacDonald's service strategy is to offer *speed, efficiency, low price,* and most important, *convenience* to the fast-food customer. The food is prepared in the same high-quality manner worldwide, and it is tasty and reasonably priced. The service level rarely varies, and the low-key decor and friendly atmosphere of each outlet remain constant.

Holiday Inn hotels. The Holiday Inn chain of hotels offers *convenience at a moderate price* for the business and middle-class traveler. The hotels are often located near the downtown or airport sections of most large to midsize cities. The rooms themselves are clean and comfortable. The chain either provides a built-in restaurant or is located near to various local eating establishments.

While the Holiday Inn may not rank among the "four star" high-class hotels in the United States, its services make it an exceptional value for the traveler. Incidentally, Holiday Corporation, the parent company, also owns the Embassy Suite hotels, which are quite different in their service orientation. They offer high luxury and extraspecial personal service to the upscale business traveler.

Hyatt Hotels. Like Holiday Inn, the Hyatt Hotels offer comfortable surroundings for the business traveler. The difference between the two organizations is that the Hyatt is definitely a "luxury" hotel, which prides itself on providing the best amenities to its guests. Its service strategy is to provide a luxury environment for the business traveler.

The Hyatt Regency properties are all dramatic in their architecture and opulent in their interior decor. They are also centrally located in most large cities. Hyatt management strives to offer its customers benefits designed to attract repeat business and establish brand loyalty. These services may not be offered by a hotel like the Holiday Inn, and the Hyatt hopes that the corporate customer will spend the extra money to receive the extra luxury service.

Mervyn's Department Stores. Mervyn's service strategy is to provide exceptional value to the price-oriented customer. The stores are located in most large cities, and provide quality and selection of both major brand name and generic brand clothing. Mervyn's offers a wide variety of all types of apparel for men, women, and children. The company mounts an extensive advertising campaign, using daily newspapers to distribute multipage catalogs to the public. This technique brings the customer to the store and the no-pressure sales staff and high-volume, low-cost selection contributes to the success of the organization.

Deluxe Check Printers. This company's philosophy is to provide blinding speed and efficiency to its customers. As the name suggests, Deluxe Check Printers prints checks for banks and savings and loan institutions nationwide. The company is well aware of the fact that when banking customers open a new checking account, they do not want to wait an inordinate amount of time to receive their checks. Deluxe has developed high-speed printing techniques and a reputation for accuracy in order to service its banking industry customers. We could describe the company's service strategy as an extremely fast response and a maximum convenience for its bank customers.

British Airways. British Airways, which we will discuss in greater detail in chapter 10, attributes much of its current success to its ability to respond to market research findings. British Airways has focused on four distinct areas that appeared in various marketing studies. The company has developed a service strategy based on care and concern, solving customer problems quickly and effectively, flexibility in dealing with customer needs, and fixing things that go wrong.

Country Fair Theme Park. Ron Zemke, in a case which we will discuss in greater detail in chapter 10, has worked with Country Fair to evolve a simple service strategy: to offer the customer the experience of "fun." By focusing the attention of all employees and managers on the fun factor through the four key categories of friendliness, cleanliness, service, and show, they were able to build repeat business and generate significant word-of-mouth business as well.

Santa Monica Hospital Medical Center. Karl Albrecht has worked with the top management at Santa Monica Hospital to evolve a specific service strategy based on significant market research findings that patients placed an extremely high value on certain key aspects of their personal experience with the medical staff and service people who treated them. The service strategy revolves around professional credibility, individualized attention to the patient's situation, and responsiveness to his or her expressed needs.

Here is an often misunderstood point about service strategy: factors like cleanliness, attractive physical surroundings, and the flavor of food often do not qualify as elements of a service strategy. If the customer *expects* you to have a clean hospital, you get no bonus points for cleanliness; you only get demerits if it is *not* clean. In such a case, cleanliness is a *minimum requirement to compete*, not a strategy element. If all the other hospitals are dirty, then cleanliness might offer a competitive edge. If the other hospitals are clean, yours had better be clean, too.

In some particular service strategies, such as those used by very up-scale hotels, factors like cleanliness and food quality are essential to success, but they are only "adequacy" factors. They must be present for the real service strategy to work. This strategy must provide an appeal beyond the customer's normal expectations. Of course, not everyone in the country wants to pay the prices for up-scale services. Not everyone can. The market for most services is segmented into at least three levels: price-oriented, value-oriented, and quality-oriented.

A price-oriented buyer usually has a limited disposable income and must make the most of it. He or she would dearly love to stay at one of Holiday Corporation's Crowne Plaza hotels or an Embassy Suite, but must instead settle for a Hampton Inn. This is why Holiday Corporation offers a complete line of choices.

The value-oriented buyer has more disposable income and

more buying flexibility, but still prefers to make choices based on the trade-off between cost and value. This buyer might choose a top-of-the-line restaurant to celebrate an anniversary or other special occasion, but wouldn't go there just for a night out.

The quality-oriented buyer is a different breed. He or she occupies a socioeconomic niche that confers the freedom to choose among the best hotels, restaurants, and vacations on the market. While not necessarily extravagant in personal tastes, this buyer wants top quality and can put up the money to get it.

This differentiation in buying preferences can show up in some unexpected places. For example, even though there is a hue and cry in the land about outrageous medical care costs, some hospitals are doing a strong business by appealing to up-scale customers. Specially equipped private rooms, extra services like high-fi systems and video cassette recorders, and live-in accommodations for visiting relatives and friends all appeal to the more affluent patient.

YOUR SERVICE STRATEGY IS NOT ON THE LIST

The chances are high that none of the examples cited above are just right for your particular business. The service strategy right for you depends on your market—on the needs, expectations, and motivations of your customers, on the strength of your main competitors, on your particular business mission, on the guiding principles and values of your company, and on the special point of view you have about your possibilities.

Finding your best service strategy may be a difficult and challenging experience, or it may be completely straightforward. In any case the degree to which you have clarified your strategy, made it simple and easy to understand, and taught it to the leaders and workers of your organization is the degree to which you will be able to move your company toward the implementation of the strategy.

THE DIFFERENCE BETWEEN PRODUCT AND CUSTOMER NEEDS

Up to this point, we have been talking almost exclusively about ways to fill expressed customer needs. In almost every workshop we have conducted on the service management concept, there comes a point when someone in the room becomes uncomfortable with our insistence on this obsession and challenges it. The objection usually goes something like this:

> Wait a minute! Sure, the customer has a *role* in shaping our services, but there are a lot of times when the consumer just doesn't know what he needs. There are any number of business successes built on products and services the consumer didn't have the slightest idea he needed until we told him he needed it.

Fair enough and true! There is a bounty of examples of products and services apparently *inventing needs* instead of the other way around. The telephone, automobile, credit card, and labor union are all inventions that might be cited as examples of products and services for which there was no demand until they were invented. Throw in the airplane, representative democracy, the stock market, the personal computer, Post-It Notes, and the written word for good measure, and we have the making of an interesting debate about the wellsprings of innovation.

For our part we readily admit and acknowledge that it is possible to bring something totally new into being—something for which there is no obvious and pressing demand—and to successfully take it to the marketplace. Our point is that it is a difficult and risky task. Innovation that is technology- or business-driven, as opposed to customer-driven, is doubly difficult to bring to life. Take something as seemingly logical and important as the automobile seatbelt. It makes sense and *should* be accepted by the consumer. But the fact of the matter is that if the seatbelt were just another product and not a controversial life-and-death issue, and if the consumer were to simply accept or reject it on the face of its advertised features and benefits, it would have died off decades ago.

Perhaps a perfect example of what happens when innovation clashes with consumer need, is the struggle being waged by American banks to replace human with automated tellers. The conflict is easy to understand. According to the Bank Administration Institute, the average banking transaction conducted by a flesh-and-blood teller costs 52 cents. The same transaction conducted by an automated teller machine, or ATM, costs 21 cents. The banks desperately want us to forgo high touch for high tech. The problem is that we don't want to. Time and again, market research studies tell the same tale: convenience, fast service, account security, personal attention, and contact with knowledgeable personnel are our personal banking hot buttons.

Although the United States has been blanketed with ATMs—about $1 billion-worth over the last 10 years—only about one third of us put hand to a keyboard and punched in a personal identification number (PIN) to fulfill our financial-transaction needs in 1984. According to one study, fewer than 10 percent of the over 45 billion bank transactions made in that period were conducted by computer; all the rest were handled by check.

The banks have hardly given up and are still striving mightily to win us over to ATMs. Over the years we have been offered bonuses and incentives; we have had our names entered into lotteries for using them and been offered trips to Hawaii for persistence. A recent *Wall Street Journal* story chronicled the most recent of these machinations. Pittsburgh National Bank sent $2 checks to thousands of customers; the checks were good only if deposited in their accounts through an ATM. Cleveland's Ameritrust established itself as the giveaway leader through a contest that awarded Apple computers, color television sets, and microwave ovens to ATM users.

On the other side of the street in Cleveland, the strategy has been to make teller access harder. At the Central National Bank of Cleveland, customers must insert their ATM cards in a terminal at a teller window to summon a teller. Colonial Bank in Waterbury, Connecticut, in the words of *Journal* reporter Daniel Hertzberg, goes so far as to try "tugging at people's heartstrings" by offering to donate a nickel to a children's cancer fund every time someone opts for an ATM over a live teller. All that movement and muscle, and still two thirds of us say, "No need—no sale," to the offer.

Will the banks prevail? Will we eventually accept ATMs as an effective way to do our personal banking business? In business as in poker, never bet against the bank. Don't forget that the banking industry is based on the proposition that "*Time* Marches On," and so far it has. And as *The Wall Street Journal* story pointed out, Citibank has already made ATM users of over half its retail customer base.

Whether the banks win over our hearts and minds or not so that we shall eventually concede to let our fingers do the banking is not really the point. The lesson to be learned is in the cost of the struggle. Creating a need and a demand where there is none—worse yet—convincing consumers to do something they don't want to do and can't imagine that they will enjoy doing, all this takes three things: time, money, and more money. And as the folks at the IRS and Selective Service can attest, an occasional act of Congress thrown in for good measure doesn't hurt. Finding a need and filling it are cheaper and easier if not as entrepreneurially exciting.

6

Building the Service System

> The ability to understand the customer's needs and wants can be
> summed up in a simple phrase: "Always be learning."
> —*Karl Albrecht/Ron Zemke*

Now it is time to explore another critical element of the service
triangle, the *system.* The service system is all of the apparatus,
physical and procedural, that the service people have at their dis-
posal to meet the customer's needs. In this chapter we will describe
a rationale for being good by design—an approach to designing
the total service system in such a way as to maximize its effectiveness. For the next few pages we invite you to think in systems
terms. We are going to explore the critical elements of service
system analysis and design.

What are the components of any service system? In a theme
park, for example, much of the service system consists of the
physical facilities: the grounds, the various attractions, the food
service setup, the ticket sales operation, the cleanup operation,
and all the other activities that make the park run. The system
also includes less visible activities: for example, food procurement,
and handling and storage. Maintenance and repair of the facilities
is also a crucial part of the service system. Even though the customer never sees these and other key parts of the system, they
are essential to delivering the service.

The key success factor, where the service system is concerned,
is the "customer-friendly" system. Service systems that are low
on the friendliness scale tend, by their very design, to subordinate
convenience and ease of access *for the customer* in favor of the
convenience of the people who work within the system. A customer-friendly system, on the other hand, is one whose basic design makes things easy for the customer. The design of an effective
service system actualizes the service priorities spelled out by the

service strategy. It is a customer-friendly system because it starts and ends with customer needs, expectations, and buying motivations.

NEEDS VERSUS EXPECTATIONS

We have previously emphasized the importance of understanding the customer's buying logic. We need to find out what the customer wants—what he or she will buy and won't buy. We use two distinct attributes of consumer psychology, *needs* and *expectations,* to describe the demand component of the service package. The distinction is important, because the two are as different as they are crucial to the ultimate consumer judgement of service satisfaction. An organization's service package must contain not only what its customers need but also what they expect if they are to be pleased with the offered service.

Customer needs have an unsettling way of not staying satisfied for very long. Fads come and go, trends rise and fall, and new ways of living and doing business emerge. As people get older and the population undergoes noticeable demographic shifts, it becomes necessary to rethink products, services, and whole markets.

People also become familiar with products and services they once considered new or novel. F. Stewart DeBruicker and Gregory L. Summe refer to "the customer experience factor."[1] Their analysis suggests that the more experience customers have with a product or service, the more discerning they become about their own needs and the variety of ways available for meeting those needs. They add that customers are not all alike, and that their needs and motivations change as their experience with your product or service increases. We can think in terms of two distinct types of customer: the inexperienced generalist, who is naive about your product or service, and the experienced specialist and sophisticated buyer, who is quite familiar with your product or service.

As a person progresses along the scale of experience from inexperienced generalist to experienced specialist, his or her needs begin to shift, expectations become more demanding, and evaluations become more critical. Depending on the nature of the product or service, it may pay to try to "tailor" your service offering to more than one level of familiarity and experience. In this way you can appeal to beginners without leaving out the more seasoned users, and vice versa.

Our *expectations* in service situations also clearly influence our perception of satisfaction. The expectations set for us by an organization we wish to deal with, and the way these are met, determine whether we will do business with the organization again. The leaders of any organization need to consider carefully the service expectations they set.

European service management expert Richard Normann has this to say about reactions when perceived expectations are and are not met:

> It is when the service package does not contain what we have been led to expect by previous experience or by promises, that we complain. As consumers we are in fact so guided by habit or expectation that we hardly notice normal, good, efficient service. If we go to a restaurant, we expect the food to be excellent and the service courteous. We expect an airline to keep the waiting time at the check-in desk down to a reasonable level.
>
> When normal good service is provided, we accept it without a second thought. We notice the lack of good service, or service which falls below what we have come to expect, much more than we notice normal, satisfactory service. We (generally) accept being treated to higher standards than we had come to expect, but if the service falls short of our expectations in some respects, we immediately register the fact and react to it.[2]

We don't entirely agree with Normann that good service largely goes unnoticed. We certainly agree that one of the difficulties with service is that obtaining reliable feedback on the quality of service can be difficult. There is a greater likelihood that people will tell us when their expectations are not reached, rather than when they have been met. It may be tempting to overreact when the customer is unhappy with some part of the service function. When the only news we get is the bad news, we may have a difficult time perceiving that any part of what we are doing is acceptable. We need to take care not to allow this factor to distort the design of a new service.

Let's stop for a moment and consider how people judge service. While a crossed expectation may prompt the customer to speak up, over the long haul that same customer will judge the service of an organization on the basis of all of the factors taken together. Our judgements about overall service quality tend to be a composite of the interactions—the moments of truth—with the service provider as well as our reactions to the tangibles involved.

Some people suggest a rough rule of thumb for measuring service: "It takes twelve 'pluses' to make up for one 'minus.'" Others dispute the quasi-scientific implications of such numerical factors, and contend that different factors carry different weights in the overall evaluation of whether the service is acceptable and the encounter worth repeating. The final lesson is that raised expectations are often difficult to reduce. Services offered, either peripheral or core, must actually be deliverable by the service organization.

THE SERVICE PACKAGE: DECIDING WHAT TO OFFER TO WHOM

One of the most helpful concepts in service management is the notion of the *service package*. This term which originated in Scandinavia, is widely used there in evaluating service levels. Service management experts vary in the definitions they offer, but most of them agree on something roughly like this:

> The service package is the sum total of the goods, services and experiences offered to the customer.

It may help to think of the service strategy, the service package, and the service system as interrelated in the following way:

SERVICE STRATEGY →	SERVICE PACKAGE →	SERVICE SYSTEM
Defines the business	Defines the offer	Delivers the service

The service package concept provides a framework for thinking systematically about the delivery system. Your service package follows logically from your service strategy. It constitutes the basic value you deliver. Your service system then follows from the definition of the service package.

There is no real mystery to this package. In most organizations there is already an existing set of goods, services, and experiences. Except for rare cases, service packages start small and evolve over the years. If they need rethinking, however, it helps to go back to first principles and think through the entire design in the light of the service strategy.

Richard Normann of the Service Management Group in Paris likes to distinguish between *core services*—the big benefits the consumer is looking for—and *peripheral services*—the little things, or added bonuses, that go along with the big benefits. A similar distinction, used in Scandinavia, is between the *primary service package* and the *secondary service package*.

The primary service package is the centerpiece of your service offering. It is your basic reason for being in business. Without the primary service package, your business enterprise would make no sense. It needs to reflect the overriding logic of your service strategy, and it needs to offer a natural, compatible set of goods, services, and experiences that go together in the customer's mind to form an impression of high value.

Your *secondary service package* needs to support, complement, and *add value* to your primary service package. The secondary package should not be a hodge podge of "extras," thrown in with no forethought. All of these secondary service features should provide "leverage," that is, help build up the value of the total package in the customer's eyes.

Understanding the potentially synergistic relationship between the primary service package and the secondary service package can point the way to some creative and effective approaches to the design of service.

In a primary-care hospital, for example, the primary service to the patient-customer consists of lodging, nursing care, and the administering of medical treatments ordered by the attending physician. Secondary, or peripheral services, include the comfort and convenience elements such as the telephone and TV, the visitor convenience provisions, the gift shop, the pharmacy and all the rest.

In a hotel the primary service package includes a clean, properly equipped room. The secondary service package includes extra services such as wake-up calls, morning coffee and newspaper, laundry or shoe-shining service, and transportation to and from the airport.

The distinction between primary elements of service and secondary elements can often be crucial. When two or more companies are competing in roughly the same market for the business of the same customer, and they are offering the same basic services, the only way any of these companies can gain a competitive edge is by offering added value.

Once a core service has done its job, that is, met the primary need, the peripherals of the service package take over as the key factors in the customer's decision. In many situations the only possible difference between competitors lies with these peripherals. Often the basic products and services offered by company

A and company B are virtually indistinguishable from one another in the eyes of the consumer. The customer uses the peripheral features to judge the relative value of the products. The strongest company in the marketplace may turn out to be the one that offers the best-designed package of peripherals.

Hotels, for example, are experimenting with various peripheral service options and trying to find the ones that can make a difference to the customer who has been thoroughly conditioned to expect the basic elements of the core service package. Holiday Inn's up-scale Crowne Plaza hotels, for example, offer personal computers on an hourly rental basis to business travelers.

Some banks are catering to senior-citizen customers by providing lounge areas, free coffee, and investment clubs that serve as meeting places. More and more hospitals are setting up weight-control clinics, prenatal classes for prospective mothers and fathers, and physician-referral services for patients who need treatment but have no family physician.

Another useful notion in the design of the service package is the difference between *explicit benefits* and *implicit benefits*. An explicit benefit is one that is easily noticeable, such as the highly attentive personal service provided by a world-class restaurant. An implicit benefit might be a more subtle aspect of the service, such as when the maître-d' calls you by name and remembers your food preferences when you take your associates or clients to the restaurant for lunch. Good food and good service are explicit benefits. Being known by name at a top restaurant is an implicit benefit. In some cases the implicit benefits offered by the peripheral service package may outweigh the significance of the explicit benefits of the core package.

Defining the service package calls for a clear understanding of the wants, needs, and expectations of the customer, a clear strategy for delivering service, and a great deal of creative thought and market judgement. Once you have a clear definition of the service package, you are in a position to approach the design or redesign of the service system with a view toward maximizing the strength of your competitive position.

THE SERVICE SYSTEM: DOING THE RIGHT THINGS RIGHT

Traditionally, planning—in the strategic sense—has been anathema to people in charge of service systems, or at least it seems that way. Many, if not most, of the service systems we all encounter on a day-to-day basis seem intractable, unmoving, and unmovable.

For most of this century service has been an afterthought, really, in most industries. Managers have treated it alternately as a marketing gimmick or a necessary and costly evil by-product of the manufacture of goods. Service has seldom been seen as a major strategic thrust, and certainly not as a business proposition unto itself.

In the mind of the aspiring industrialist of the early 20th century, service was inseparably associated with "servileness"; with maids, butlers, bellhops, coachmen, and undertakers. It was hardly the sort of thing a would-be Rockefeller, Morgan, or Carnegie would think of as a source of profit. The only awareness a true captain of industry should have of the quality of service was being on the receiving end.

Within the context of that image of service, it is small wonder that most contemporary service systems are so bad. It isn't so much that anybody purposely built them to deliver mediocre service, as that they have been intellectually abandoned and allowed to "evolve" on their own. This is a case of simple historical neglect. When you allow an organizational system to evolve on its own, you can be fairly sure it will evolve in the direction of self-convenience, becoming introverted rather than outwardly focused.

G. Lynn Shostack, senior vice president of New York's Bankers Trust Company, and an expert on service delivery, agrees with this perception of service quality. In a recent *Harvard Business Review* article she comments:

> Examples of poor service are widespread; in survey after survey, services top the list in terms of consumer dissatisfaction. Ideas like H & R Block's approach to tax preparation, the McDonald's formula for fast-food service, and Walt Disney's concept of entertainment are so few and far between that they seem to be the product of genius—a brilliant flash that can never be duplicated.[3]

The key point here is that we are entering an era of unprecedented demand for high-quality service on a worldwide scale, and most of the service systems we must depend on to fulfill this growing demand make about as much sense as a wild bramble bush. They follow no rhyme nor reason; they make no operational, economic, or logical sense at all. They are, in a word, unplanned.

It is a striking feature of the well-planned and executed service system that the service itself seems simple and uncomplicated. The system works so well and the service is produced so effortlessly that the "system" is nearly invisible. For example, if you ever visited one of the large, modern theme parks, you have probably marveled at the cleanliness of the grounds and the beauty and bounty of the flowers and shrubs. You may have said something like, "My, my. I wish our yard (city/company) could be as spotless and well-groomed as this. How do they do it? They must have really good people doing the work."

Not so. In fact, Disney, Six Flags, Great Adventures, and most of the other well-known theme parks do what they do with minimum-wage employees, the same teenagers we can't even get to pick up their socks. How do they do it? Put something in the water? Threaten them? Not at all.

There is nothing magic or superhuman about it. For example, think about the flowers, shrubs, and trees you found so attractive. Most theme parks have a large, well-trained horticultural staff that spends many hours tending the flora. As a guest, you never see these persons at work because you aren't supposed to. They do most of their work at night when the park is closed to the public.

Cleanliness involves a similar sleight of hand: it is going on right in front of you all the time, but you hardly notice it. A swarm of youngsters is constantly floating through assigned areas of the park, picking up papers and mopping up spills. In the best-known of the theme parks, the Disney properties, there are special vacuum-powered trash transport tubes located all about the grounds. As a guest, you will never see an employee rolling away a giant cart bearing a smelly mass of accumulated trash.

In addition, there is a sort of industrywide behavioral norm at work. Everyone who works in a theme park, from the president of the corporation to the newest hot dog vendor, is expected to pick up trash wherever it is spotted. Out of sight, out of mind. They keep it out of sight, and it never crosses your mind that somebody has to get rid of all that trash. The point is that although the best theme parks are almost always shiny-clean, odorfree, and pretty to see, it is planning, forethought, and follow-through that keeps them that way, not superhuman effort.

Contrast this with the *unplanned* service system, which is easy to spot. Unplanned systems share one common, unmistakable characteristic: they seem to operate solely for the convenience of the organization and the employees of the system, not for delivering service or promoting service satisfaction among their clientele.

Here is a simple "litmus test" you can perform that will tell you whether the systems in the organization you are dealing with are "designed" or "evolved." The next time you telephone an organization, make two measurements. First, count the number of interdepartmental transfers you go through before you get anything resembling help. Next, count the number of people who explain to you why they can't help you because the thing you want to know or have done is the responsibility of sales, credit, operations, payroll, public relations, or some other unit, or because the person involved is at this very minute out to lunch with somebody *really* important and will be in later if you want to call back.

Rationally, of course, we all know that the goal is first and foremost to provide value to the customer. But there is, in most organizations, a conspiracy of accolades and incentives that tie people to the rules of the system first and the needs of the customer second. This, by the way, may account for much of the tension between "inside" people and "outside" people.

Inside people are often suspicious of outside people, especially sales people. Aside from looking like professional fancy dressers, high rollers, and smooth talkers, salespeople seem to be forever hustling the insiders for special treatment and favors for their customers. To the insider, this attitude seems to verge on disloyal, if not downright traitorous, behavior.

Examples abound of systems that serve the organization first: hospital admission systems focused on payment rather than pain; car repair operations concerned with responsibility and warranty rather than repair; bank loan systems that make the customer feel like a crook or a deadbeat rather than a business partner; government bureaus preoccupied with forms at the expense of function; and computer departments concerned with machinery and methods rather than timely information.

In order to make a service system truly customer-friendly, we must design it or redesign it in a comprehensive way. Richard Normann, who was closely associated with the SAS story, makes this observation on the successful service system as a model from which others can learn:

> In practice, it is difficult in a service operation to distinguish clearly between the service, the process of providing the service, and the system for delivering it. . . . (The key to designing a successful service) is, briefly: the ability to think in wholes. . . . [T]he integration of structure and process is indispensable to the creation of effective service systems.[4]

Lynn Shostack adds:

There are several reasons for the lack of analytical service systems design. Services are unusual in that they have impact but no form. Like light, they can't be physically stored or possessed and their consumption is often simultaneous.[5]

Shostack contends, however, that this quicksilver nature of service is no excuse for being haphazard or arbitrary in setting up the systems. She adds, "There is no way to ensure quality or uniformity in the absence of a detailed design."

DESIGNING SERVICES IN A SYSTEMATIC FASHION

It becomes more and more evident that services can and must be systematically designed if they are to be reliably delivered. While that may raise the specter of assembly-linelike, engineered work with no room for individual style and personality, that need not be the case. The purpose of designing services in a systematic fashion, to us, is just the opposite of dehumanization. The goal of systematic design is to minimize the forms, procedures, and folderol standing between the service and the customer. At the same time the service designer must always be concerned that the consumer receives the service he or she expects from the organization and at a cost the organization can profit from.

As we have pointed out, a service, because of its intangibility, can't be prototyped, wind-tunnel tested, or debugged the way a new typewriter, automobile, or piece of software can. The testing of a service idea frequently requires an expensive and very public market-testing phase to demonstrate its worth. If the service fails to fly or, worse yet, proves attractive to the public but disappoints because of a weak delivery system, the organization can suffer a loss of image that affects consumer confidence in *other* services and products. Some organizations are so sensitive to this problem that they would rather go to the expense of establishing a separate entity—frequently a new small company—to have a go at the new service idea than risk the parent company's reputation. The strategy certainly encourages the would-be entrepreneurs in the organization, but it does little to take the risk out of the actual venture.

What is helpful, is the emergence of techniques for building services on paper that allow the sort of predevelopment troubleshooting that goes on in the development of physical products. This developing art/science of service engineering is so new that it really hasn't an agreed-upon name, much less an established body of principles and techniques. The few practitioners who realize they are onto something describe their work by its similarity to the more familiar operations analysis tools and techniques: work flow design, time and motion study, PERT and GANIT, and so forth.

Indeed, some services are so simple that they can be easily described using common job-analysis techniques. The following simple narrative is an adequate explanation of what the jewelry store clerk must do when a customer comes in looking for service.

PROCEDURE FOR RECEIVING MERCHANDISE FOR REPAIR

When a customer brings an item in for repair, you must first verify that the merchandise was purchased from Clunkies. Acceptable proof of purchase are a canceled check, a charge card receipt, or a cash sale receipt.

If the Item Was Purchased at Clunkies: fill out a pink receipt, place the item in an Item-for-Repair Envelope, staple the pink or top copy to the envelope, and give the remaining or white copy to the customer.

If the Item Was Not Purchased at Clunkies: fill out a blue receipt, place the item in an Item-for-Repair Envelope, staple the blue or top copy to the envelope, and give the remaining or green copy to the customer.

When the Customer Has Left: enter the transaction in the department log book, and place the item in the department safe.

This description of the service procedure is perfectly usable, if rather vanilla, and could be used to check the procedures with other jewelry department managers for adequacy and accuracy, and used to train clerks from. Even if we add 20 or 30 more duties to the service clerk's job, this approach to detailing the individual services would probably be perfectly adequate. Add in some simple time standards, and we could easily cost out the service clerk portion of the actual cost of repairing jewelry at Clunkies.

Many, if not most, services are substantially more complex and time consuming than those performed by the Clunkies clerk. Even a task as simple as pumping gas at a full service filling station is a fairly complex operation. Figure 6–1 is part of the task breakdown of that job.

Because of the complexity of the station attendant job—a complexity added primarily by the number of decisions the job tasks entail—the service is much more easily understood and reviewed in algorithmic or flow-chart fashion. Notice that as the number of task variations goes up, the job becomes increasingly more difficult to "fix" for costing purposes.

FIGURE 6–1 Part of a Task Breakdown Chart for the Job of Service Station Attendant

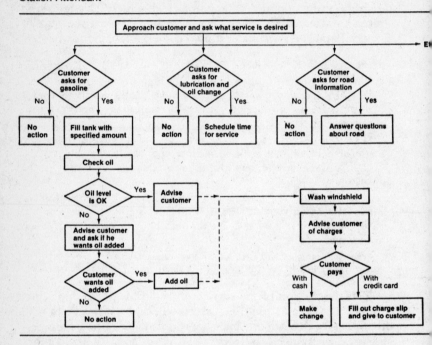

Note: Diamond-shaped figures represent possible conditions; rectangles represent actions.

SOURCE: Reprinted, by permission of the publisher, from JOB ANALYSIS: METHODS AND APPLICATIONS, by Ernest J. McCormick, p. 100 © 1979 AMACOM, a division of American Management Associations, New York. All rights reserved.

The simple act of representing this level of complexity in a form that can be looked at in toto gives the designer an opportunity to ask questions about the value some of the task clusters add to the service in the consumer's eyes.

Figure 6–2 is a Decision Analysis Table for the seemingly simple act of cashing a check—from the tellers point of view. When we consider that tellers not only cash checks, but take deposits for a variety of different kinds of accounts—savings, money market, Christmas Club, and so forth—as well as accept payments, cut money orders, and sell travelers checks, it becomes obvious why bank operations people are so enamored with the Automated Teller Machine.

One of the most sophisticated and promising approaches to service engineering and design is an approach that yields what Shostack calls a service blueprint.[6] Developing a service blueprint allows the service designer to identify the processes involved in the delivery of the service, isolate potential failure points in the system, and establish time frames for the service delivery. This in turn allows for a systematic profitability analysis of the service. And all this takes place before the new, or proposed, service ever leaves the drawing board.

The Profitability Analysis Worksheet and Blueprint in Figure 6–3 are adapted from a 1984 *Harvard Business Review* article in which Shostack first detailed her approach. At the risk of turning this into a course in service engineering, we think it is useful to point out some of the features of the service blueprint that make it so useful to the process of designing and developing a service.

1. A service blueprint can become a lengthy document. As you can see, even as simple and straightforward a service as shoeshining can occupy several steps in a service blueprint. We once detailed the job of a first-level bank teller in a similar fashion, for the purpose of developing training. The completed job algorithm, a process-flow diagram similar to a service blueprint, covered 36 pages 11 by 18 inches.

2. The service blueprint, as opposed to a straightforward flow diagram, separates activities that can be seen by or that require participation from the customer. Likewise, materials and activities that do not directly involve the customer are accounted for, since they represent a part of the service system and hence the real cost of the service, but they are kept "offline" and out of the flow of the service delivery.

3. The service blueprint is helpful in isolating places where a current service is weak or prone to failure. By tapping the expertise of people who have worked with services similar to a service in the development stages, potential and probable service failure points can be anticipated and fail-safed or engineered around.

4. Once the blueprint has been scrutinized for completeness, and vulnerabilities have been assessed and compensated for, costing of the service and profitability analysis can begin. In the case of an existing service, the process is fairly straightforward. Stop

FIGURE 6-2 Decision Analysis Table for the Bank Teller Task—Check Cashing

Item Is	Presentor Is Customer with Checking, Savings, or Certificate of Deposit who is well known to the teller	Customer with Checking, Savings, or Certificate of Deposit who is NOT well known to the teller	Customer who has Installment Loan or Christmas Saving only	Non-Customer accompanied by a well-known Customer who has endorsed the item	Non-Customer	Non-Customer Friend or Relative of the teller
Maker's own check on Us payable to cash	TC 61 on Maker CASH	TC 61 on Maker CASH*	Not Applicable	Not Applicable	Not Applicable	Not Applicable
On Us Personal Check Payable to an individual (or to cash if presentor is other than the maker)	TC 61 on Maker CASH	TC 61 on Maker CASH*	CASH* if small. REFER if large TC 61	TC 61 on Maker CASH	REFER to Officer	REFER to Officer
Personal Check Drawn on Another Bank	TC 88 on Customer	TC 88 on Customer*	REFER to Officer	TC 88 on Customer	REFUSE Politely	REFUSE Politely
On Us Payroll Check	TC 61 on Maker CASH**	TC 61 on Maker CASH**	REFER to Officer	TC 61 on Maker CASH**	Identify and CASH** TC 61 or REFER	TC 61 on Maker CASH**
Payroll Check Drawn on Another Bank	CASH	CASH, hold if Company is Unknown	REFER to Officer	CASH	REFUSE Politely	REFUSE Politely
Insurance Draft	CASH	DEPOSIT Hold	Enter as Collection Item	REFER to Officer	REFUSE Politely	Enter as Collection Item
On Us Officers, Official, Cashiers, or Certified Check	CASH	CASH*	CASH if not Identified REFER	CASH	REFER to Officer	REFER to Officer
Officers, Official, Cashiers, or Certified Checks on another Bank	CASH	REFER to Officer	REFER to Officer	REFER to Officer	REFUSE Politely	REFUSE Politely
Government Checks	CASH	CASH*	REFER to Officer	CASH	REFUSE Politely	REFUSE Politely
On Us Money Orders	Call M.O. Department CASH if OK	Call M.O. Department CASH* if OK	Call M.O. Department CASH* if OK	Call M.O. Department CASH if OK	REFER to Officer	REFER to Officer
Other Money Orders	CASH	CASH*, hold if necessary	REFER to Officer	CASH	REFUSE Politely	REFUSE Politely
Travelers Cheques	CASH	CASH*	CASH*	CASH	CASH*	CASH

IMPORTANT: This sheet is a guide only. It is a statement of what you can attempt to do in given situations. It *IS NOT* permission to go ahead and take the action specified. It takes the bank's policy on various kinds of checks and customers. It is up to you to decide if the type of account the customer has, the identification presented, and type of check presented to you justify your taking the action permitted. Do not refer to this chart in the presence of customers, and do not use its terms or classifications in conversations with customers.

"CASH, HOLD" means to cash the item only if the customer's balance is sufficient to hold the amount of the item.

*One asterisk means that you must always identify the presenter from the signature cards, or from other positive identification if no signature is available. You must make a note of the identification used on the back of item.

**Two asterisks mean that you must verify the signatures and the authority to sign on company checks.

A Well Known customer is one whose account has been open at least one year and is trouble free. He comes in regularly, and you know his name, employment, and signature from memory. You feel that he would be able to take care of the amount of the check if it is returned.

SOURCE: Clyde Jackson, *Verbal Information Systems: A Comprehensive Guide To Writing Manuals* (Cleveland, Ohio: Association For Systems Management, 1974).

watch studies can develop standard times and deviation envelopes for the processes on the blueprint. It is possible to play "what if" games using the blueprint. Asking hypothetical questions about changes to the service and calculating the effects on the profitability work to keep interesting but unprofitable—and impossible—variations on the drawing board and out of the service delivery system.

Whether you choose to use Shostack's method, or some other, there are several additional benefits to the service delivery system diagraming process.

- Decisions about staff procurement, allocation, and development become clearer when you can see, right there in front of you, the kinds and number of people needed to operate and manage the service system.
- Considerations about where automation might save money and where personalized human contact is a must, can be pinpointed using the blueprint as a discussion focus.
- Competitive services can be studied and analyzed by diagraming them and comparing blueprints.
- Used as the focus for productivity improvement discussions, service blueprints can make employee participation much easier to develop. Employee involvement is a critical issue in decentralizing complex service decisions and in engineering out the design problems that characterize new service introductions.

Perhaps the most important benefit of applying rigorous analysis to the development and management of services and service systems is what Normann refers to as "the ability to think in terms of wholes and of the integration of structure and process." It is tools and techniques like the service blueprint that free us in that direction. The ability to conceptualize a service in a rational and manageable fashion is critical to solving the next level of problem beyond transportability, which is the problem of keeping a successful service organization on the path of continuous growth and innovation.

DESIGNING THE WORK SYSTEM

Though we have spent a full chapter discussing at length the care and feeding of the people who work the service system, it

FIGURE 6–3 Service Blueprint: Shoeshine

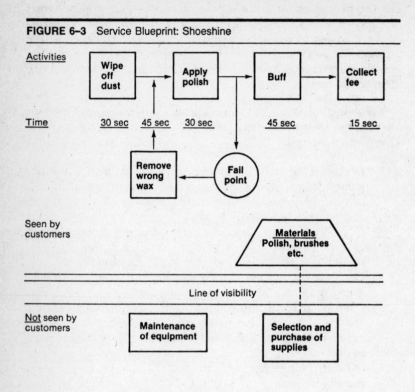

Profitability Analysis

	Execution Time		
	2 Minutes	3 Minutes	4 Minutes
Price of service	75¢	75¢	75¢
Cost of service			
Labor + 15¢/minute	30¢	45¢	60¢
Wax	5¢	5¢	5¢
Overhead, etc.	15¢	15¢	15¢
Total costs	50¢	65¢	80¢
Pre-tax profits	25¢	10¢	5¢

is appropriate to stop here and consider the relationship between the service delivery system and the management, development, motivation, and rewarding of the people who cash the checks, repair the machines, take the orders, answer the phones, book the reservations, catalog the medicines, cook the meals, and in general do the work of the service system. In most service systems the price of systems hardware is dwarfed by labor costs. Likewise, there are many more possible fail points in the people parts of most service systems than in the machine aspects. This simple dictum prompted Federal Express Company to spend $5.5 million on the *training* of station personnel prior to the introduction of Zap Mail, the organization's electrofax message system. Though the actual transmission of messages through the system is highly automated, it is Federal Express *people* who ensure that hardcopy messages are sent and received in the guaranteed two hours. The *focus* of the FEC Zap Mail service system is the customer's need to move information from A to B in a hurry, not several rooms full of computer and telecommunication equipment. Federal Express knew that, and as a result its service people were trained as carefully as the "fax" equipment was designed and built. Whether your service delivery is 99 percent automated or 100 percent face-to-face with the consumer, it is still the people who must make the service go.

Consequently, you need to think through several issues after your service is designed, debugged, and ready to move from paper to performance. The first is *measurement.* You will naturally want to or you will need to measure the performance of the service and the system. The first level of measurement you need to think through is the system performance level. How will you measure outcome? Number of shoes shined per hour? Dollars per customer? Depth of the relationship?

And how do your outcome measures relate to the subsystems or processes within the service system? What are the critical processes you need to measure? Is traffic through the door important? Should you measure opportunities as well as outcomes? Is the average length of telephone contact an important variable strongly related to the outcomes you are measuring? Is simple customer satisfaction a worthy measure? These process measures should give you indicators of how you are progressing toward achieving your desired outcomes and give you leverage—as well as ideas— for tightening standards and procedures. The important first-step question is, What are the least number of indicators you can measure, and still feel comfortable that the system has proper controls?

What are the people-performance factors that should be measured? It is important to measure people performance separately from process and system performance? It is important to measure the people performance fairly. You need to measure people on things they can directly affect, either as individuals or as a team. In a theme park, for example, gross revenues and total attendance are only indirectly related to any individual's job and are not a fair measure of, say, a parking-lot attendant's or a cashier's performance. On the other hand, guest ratings of the cleanliness of the parking lot, the weight of trash collected per shift, the friendliness or helpfulness of attendants, and the friendliness, efficiency and per transaction expenditure by cashier probably are.

Just as important as what you measure, is what you do with what you measure. To affect performance, employees must know what the measures are, what acceptable and unacceptable levels of the measure are, what they mean, and how they as individuals can affect those measures. This *feedback,* as this knowledge of performance is called by organizational psychologists, is frequently missing or, if available, never provided to people with the most influence over performance—the performers themselves.

There are varied and contradicting views on the compensation and reward of people in service systems. The primary discussion is of performance-based pay versus straight salary. Opting for one or the other does not exhaust the discussion of reward. There are both tangible and intangible, formal and informal rewards to consider. As you will see, we have frequently opted to engineer token performance-based rewards into service systems as a way of both setting expectations and rewarding performance on variables that individuals and groups of employees have influence over.

The nonproduction use of employees is another issue that needs your considered thought. Employee involvement plans are popular at the moment and many of the all-star service organizations we looked at are deeply committed to quality circles and other forms of employee involvement. Others are not. As we explore our observations, be aware that we come to this topic believing that the people closest to the work, that is, the line employees, know the most about the tasks of the job. They frequently, and especially collectively, have considerable insight into the strengths and weaknesses of the service system as a whole. And be mindful of the fact that any changes in the service and the service delivery are carried out, not by management and staff, but by the line employees. If line employees have no stake in, or commitment to, new ways of doing things, they can make it difficult to bring about change.

A FINAL ADMONITION: REMEMBER THE CUSTOMER

A final note: we began the discussion of service design, or service engineering as we sometimes call it, by pointing out that most service systems don't—service, that is. The basic problem—and the reason we believe in the value of kinds of tools we have just discussed—is that the organizations we want to serve others tend strongly toward serving themselves.

In designing services, we need to remember above all else that *our logic is not necessarily the same as the customer's logic.* As we have seen before, the customer has a special perceptual frame of reference that is unique to his or her specific needs in a specific situation. Passing through the cycle of service, the customer sees the service in terms of a total experience, not an isolated activity or set of activities. People cannot see a service system as caring and concerned if its design leads employees to focus only on the performance of "tasks" and not on value provided to the customer.

Losing sight of the customer's logic can lead your organization to become introverted. Employees who don't understand the services they deliver in holistic terms easily get caught up in methods and procedures and lose sight of the effect their organizational apparatus has on the customer. Insisting that your customers should follow complicated procedures they don't understand, insisting that the customers should learn to speak your "language," and playing departmental pinball with the customers are all sure signs that your people have lost the customer focus.

The ability to understand the customer's needs and wants, to determine the nature of the service package, and to audit the current strategy can be summed up in a simple phrase, "Always be learning." The best service strategy is the one that is constantly being questioned, challenged, refined, and improved.

Creating services that meet customer needs, designing systems and procedures that assist rather than insist, and engineering customer-contact jobs that allow the employee to work in advocacy rather than opposition to the customer's interests is, we believe, the real management challenge for the 1980s and beyond.

7

The Service People

If you're not serving the customer, you'd better be serving someone who is.

—*Karl Albrecht/Ron Zemke*

"People make the difference."

"People are our most important resource."

"The frontline people are really the ones who make us or break us."

Slogans like these are so commonplace in service industries that one tends to assume that the companies that use them must live by them, at least most of the time. On the contrary, it is quite common to find a sharp disparity between the slogans of the advertising people and the realities of the customer-contact front line.

In the unconscious view of many managers, frontline people are the *least* important ones in the organization. Frontline jobs typically draw the lowest pay, get the least training and development, have the lowest potential for growth and advancement, and have the most turnover. If the frontline people do count, you certainly couldn't prove it by examining the reward systems in most organizations.

THE LAST FOUR FEET

And yet, any rational view of managing the moments of truth tells us it is crucially important to mobilize the best energies of the people who are continually forming and reforming the customer interface. One of our colleagues, Richard Israel, who is an expert on the training and development of retail sales people, offers a useful perspective on moments of truth. He says, "In any kind of retail or service business, the factor that has the biggest effect on sales is 'the last four feet.'"

Working with a major furniture retail chain, Israel found that much of the enormous advertising investment evaporated at the moment when a customer walked into the store and encountered a nonsupportive psychological environment. "The whole purpose of advertising," says Israel, "is to get the customer to come in the front door. After that point, advertising can't do anything more for you. It's up to the people in the store to take over at the last four feet." Yet in his view all too often the salesperson loses the opportunity by failing to deal skillfully with the customer's real needs and concerns.

Because retail sales people typically receive relatively little formal training compared to people in other occupations, a large majority of them have to learn the techniques of selling more or less by accident. If they survive in the job long enough, they will learn the merchandise, prices, and other particulars of the sale. But rarely do they have a chance to learn the special social skills and personal philosophies that make for effective selling. Many retail companies might invest less money in advertising and more in developing the critical frontline skills, and still be ahead in terms of total sales and profits.

Whatever we can say about retail people we can usually say just as well about frontline people in other lines of business. It is no exaggeration to say that in the majority of service organizations, the care and feeding of frontline people could be vastly improved.

CRITICAL INCIDENTS CAN MAKE YOU OR BREAK YOU

The customer in a busy, crowded restaurant says, as the server approaches, "I'm in kind of a hurry . . .," to which the server snaps, "You'll just have to be patient, *sir*. I'm working as fast as I can. As you can see, there are a lot of other people ahead of you." They end up in a silent, cold, perfunctory transaction, with no warmth, no humor, and no tip. Here is a critical incident—a moment of truth gone sour.

The customer's next sentence, had the server not interrupted him, was going to be, "What could I order that would only take a few minutes to get?" Intending no criticism, the customer was only trying to communicate his particular needs. He ended up thinking, "I wish I had gone somewhere else. I sure will, next time."

Neither person in this episode was necessarily right or wrong, but nevertheless the situation went off the track. Ultimately, however, the service establishment loses, because the customer may never come back. Moments of truth like these can have a big effect on business.

If we think back to the concept of the cycle of service, we can try to relate the customer's conception of what's happening to the service person's conception. Such conceptions may be vastly different, and indeed they are *likely* to be different, because each of them has his or her own distinct focus of attention, need system, and set of priorities.

Some moments of truth are more telling than others, more critical to the customer's evaluation. The moment when a customer first sets foot inside the hotel; when the service manager at the repair shop presents the bill; when the physician's receptionist first greets the patient-customer—these are all leverage points. If handled well—if *managed*—they can strengthen the image of the service establishment in the customer's mind. If handled clumsily, as they often are when they go *unmanaged*, they can create apprehension, animosity, and negative expectations.

Again thinking about the cycle of service, we can diagram the customer's chain of experiences from the very beginning to its nominal completion, and we can identify the moments of truth at each stage. The most telling of the moments of truth are what we are calling here the critical incidents. It makes good sense to manage all the moments of truth, and it makes even more sense to single out the most critical of them for special attention.

THE IMPORTANCE OF CUSTOMER-ORIENTED FRONTLINE PEOPLE

It seems obvious that for a service organization to thrive, the frontline people need to operate with a consistently high level of concern about, and attention to, the needs of the customers. Obvious or not, one doesn't have to look very far to find abundant examples of a lack of customer orientation in a variety of businesses. If service people are unfriendly, unhelpful, uncooperative, or uninterested in the customer's needs, the customer tends to project that same attitude onto the organization as a whole. Paraphrasing Jan Carlzon's haunting words: "To the customer, *you* are XYZ Company."

Visualize the following scene: a man walks into the men's clothing department of a large department store, possibly looking for a particular item or possibly just to browse. Within 10 seconds of his entry into the department, a salesman descends on him like a wolf guarding its territory. "Hi, there. How are you today? Is there anything I can help you with?" The aggressive eye contact, the well-practiced singsong delivery, the self-assured manner all say to the customer, "I'm the one who's in control here."

Perhaps some men like to be approached this way, but the majority seem to find this overly familiar, dominating approach offensive. In the majority of cases like this, the last four feet blow the sale. Unless the customer really needs a particular item or happens to spot something of interest, he is likely to brush off the salesperson politely and hurry on. This type of interaction seems to be more common among men than among women.

Now consider the following alternative. A man wanders into the clothing department and looks around tentatively at the bewildering array of suits and sport jackets. There are different racks with different styles and different prices. The salesman approaches him tentatively, maintains a social distance of about 10 feet, and asks, "Would you like me to point out your size, sir?" The customer replies, "Yes, please." The salesman asks his size and shows him to the racks containing suits that fit him.

This represents astute judgement on the part of the salesman. He realizes that many men don't shop for suits very often, and the typical man walking into a suit department doesn't know where to begin looking at the choices. Many men don't realize that it is the custom to arrange suits strictly according to sizes (a practice which might deserve reconsideration). The salesman has done something helpful without being perceived as aggressive. He has created a comfort situation for the customer, and paved the way for possible further interaction, advice, a try-on, and possibly a sale.

Many psychologists and sociologists contend that these miniature episodes between human beings, going on thousands of times every day, recapitulate our basic interactions as animal creatures. The study of *proxemics*, which deals with nonverbal communication, spatial context, and "body language," has much to say about human interaction in commercial contact situations.

Poorly trained or untrained frontline people usually have no choice but to work out whatever methods they can to help them sell. Unfortunately, many of the things they try don't work very well, and there is no one to help them learn. The standard philosophy in most sales occupations is that aggressiveness is all-important. Consequently, a salesperson who doesn't know much about the psychology of selling can only resort to aggressive approaches. Better training and better orientation to the selling situation can help salespeople produce much higher volumes than simply leaving them with the "I-can-sell-anybody-anything" attitude.

It should go without saying that service people need to have a certain level of maturity and social skills to do an effective job. Yet it is remarkably common to find downright toxic people placed in frontline contact jobs, even crucially important jobs. One situation that occurs disturbingly often deserves recognition as a bona fide syndrome of low service quality: the "battle-ax receptionist" syndrome. A customer walks into the front lobby of the building, wanting to know where to go or whom to visit. The person who handles this moment of truth is Gravel Gerty (females are usually the ones shunted into jobs like these). She is unfriendly, short-tempered, and irritable. She treats visitors like pests.

Gerty has been with the company for over 20 years and has worked for just about every manager in the place at some time or other. They have been passing her around from department to department, and somebody finally had a bright idea: "Let's put her out in the reception lobby. That way she won't bother anybody." She doesn't bother anybody inside the building, but she plays havoc with the impressions people have of the company.

To make matters worse, they may have combined the job of receptionist with the job of switchboard operator. Gerty does both—poorly. She knows, of course, that she is considered excess baggage by the various people in charge, and is hostile about it. Instead of confronting her with her poor performance and providing developmental opportunities for her, the managers have been shuffling her around the organization for years. They don't realize it, but they have put her in exactly the position where she can do the most damage.

There are too many people in service jobs who should never have been placed there from the start. Because of the prevailing impression among managers that anybody can do a typical customer-contact job, selection and training tend to receive little emphasis. Low-paying jobs such as switchboard operator, receptionist, and counter worker don't usually require great technical expertise or product knowledge. Consequently, it is common practice to place minimum-wage, minimally qualified people in these positions, which all too often are critical-incident positions.

Quite a few people who lack the temperament, maturity, social skills, and tolerance for frequent human contact make up the characteristic profile of a skilled service person. Often people of this kind fall prey to the personal pressures of the day-to-day contact situation, and become toxic toward their customers. *Contact overload* is a recognizable psychological syndrome experienced by frontline people who either can't handle extensive human contact or get too much of it under some circumstances. The result can often be a form of masked hostility that shows up in *robotization* of the job ("Thank-you-have-a-nice-day—NEXT!") or in petty forms of one-upping directed at the customer.

For example, the overstressed, robotized, misplaced restaurant server may bring the customer a Mexican dish with melted cheese, and then "forget" to tell the customer the plate is fresh out of the oven and too hot to touch. A shop clerk may deliberately withhold a bit of useful information that would be helpful to the customer in making a buying decision. One cannot prove that the service rendered is necessarily "bad," but it lacks the element of willingness to do something for the customer as a person.

Officiousness is also a problem in some settings, such as in hospitals and government offices and on airplanes. The nurse's aide who leans out through the partially opened door, brandishing a clipboard, and barks the last name of the patient-customer is hardly communicating a service orientation. The message is, "I'm in charge here, and there isn't going to be any nonsense." Similar to this is the airline flight attendant who adopts a critical-parent demeanor and treats each passenger like a child.

On the other hand, consider the following episode described by one of our colleagues, Jay Hall. Hall found himself standing out in the parking lot of a hotel one afternoon, along with many of the other guests, watching the fire department put out a small grease fire that had broken out in the building. Somehow in the melee, the catering staff had managed to set up coffee service on a table in the parking lot.

The guests were standing around enjoying coffee, waiting to find out what would happen next. In keeping with the rather light-hearted attitude prevailing in the situation, Hall wisecracked as he came to the coffee pot, "What? No cream?" The young man serving the coffee looked startled and said, "Just a minute!" Right away, he dashed back into the smoke-filled kitchen and came out two minutes later with a pitcher of cream. "Now that," says Hall, "is what I call a service attitude."

Of course, that isn't the kind of thing you can specifically teach someone to do in a service business, but you can create the conditions so that your employees are ready, willing, and able to go that extra four feet.

We find inspiring examples of this service attitude in nonservice businesses as well. In the spring of 1984, when floods hit the Northeast, New England Business Services, a supplier of computer forms, sent telegrams to all their customers, asking, in effect, "Can we help?" They offered to replace at no charge any forms inventory that may have been lost or damaged.

This same attitude about the extra mile—or four feet—motivated Deluxe Check Printers in the aftermath of a flood at their own plant in Kansas City. The company flew every available Kansas City employee to its headquarters plant in St. Paul, Minnesota. There they operated the St. Paul plant on an extra shift, working at night to print check orders for their Kansas City customers. The company kept at it until the Kansas City plant was ready to resume operations. Though the story of this commandotype operation is well known within the company, customers never detected a break in service and never knew of the incident.

THE SERVICE CULTURE

The concept of corporate culture is widely discussed these days, and rightly so. Of all the things we have said and will say about the management of service, the most important will be this: Unless the shared values, norms, beliefs, and ideologies of the organization—the organization's culture—are clearly and consciously focused on serving the customer, there is virtually no chance that the organization will be able to deliver a consistent quality of service and develop a sustained reputation for service.

We have said that clear performance standards are important—and they are. We have said that a sensitive and efficient feedback system is important—and it is. We have emphasized the importance of a clearly defined service package, a good delivery system, proper training, and good management. And these are just as important as they can be. But unless the culture of the organization supports and rewards attention to customer needs, service will get no more than lip service over the long run.

Carve that in stone. Knit it into a sampler. However you do it, you must make sure that you carry with you, every working hour—the notion that your job and your part of the organization exist because of and for the customer. If you don't believe that and act on it, others in the organization won't either.

It is very easy to believe in the importance of service to the customer and the impact of the culture, and yet not believe that *your* role in the game "counts." If you are the president of the company, it is easy to tell yourself, "But I am at the helm. I hardly ever see a customer anymore. I only see bankers, managers, and stockholders."

A staff person can with equal ease rationalize that "I am just a cog in the middle of the machine. I just do data processing—buy merchandise—conduct training—cut the payroll—I never see a customer. I have no part in the customer-service thing." And it is equally easy for the clerks, telephone operators, salespeople, and field repair people to find a way to say, "Who, me? I don't have any influence over how this outfit treats customers. I just follow the rules right here in the rule book." Satisfaction of customer needs is either everyone's business or it might as well be no one's business; that's the way it will be transacted. And the "feel" of who is in charge of the customer's needs is very much a belief that rests in the culture of the organization. That's the way it works at IBM, that's the way they think at Disney, and that's the way they do business at American Express. And as a result, that's the way it *is*.

All that may sound a bit too saccharine; too much "Mom's apple pie." We can certainly understand the skepticism. But it is true just the same: if your organization's culture doesn't show that service is the most important thing you can offer the customer, it isn't.

Vijay Sathe is a Harvard Business School professor who has studied the effects of culture on such organizational processes as communication, cooperation, commitment to goals, decision making, and implementation. He cautions that a strong—in his words "thick"—corporate culture, the kind Disney, Am Ex, and IBM are touted to have, is a double-edged sword:

> It is an asset because shared beliefs ease and economize communications, and shared values generate higher levels of cooperation and commitment than is otherwise possible. This is highly efficient. . . . Culture is a liability when the shared beliefs and values are not in keeping with the needs of the organization, its members, and other constituencies.[1]

One of the strongest service cultures we know of pervades the American Express Travel Related Services Company—the part of Am Ex that handles travel, traveler's checks, and credit cards. Lou Gerstner, Jr., chairman and chief executive of the company, is good at standing before a group of TRS employees and hammering home the message. Here is an excerpt from one of his messages to a luncheon of TRS frontline troops:

> Superior service to our global customers is neither a simple slogan to be periodically recited nor an ancient tradition to be abstractly venerated: It is our daily mandate which we must execute flawlessly all over the world. Moreover, because our consumer franchise depends so heavily on unexcelled customer service, our company's internal value system must emphasize the primacy of our dealings with clients above all other business priorities. In my mind—and I believe in the minds of our customers—second-class treatment from American Express equates to intolerable treatment. So perfection— or something very close to perfection—is the only acceptable daily standard for our customer service in TRS.[2]

What makes this message interesting to us, other than the simple fact that we think it is a great sentiment to be expressing, is that it was delivered at the company's 1983 Great Performers Award luncheon. The Great Performers, if you haven't guessed, are those people in TRS who have distinguished themselves by exceptional service to the customer in the past year—anywhere in the world.

What does it take to be a Great Performer at American Express? Some of the Am Ex stories are almost unbelievable. Meriam Troken, who runs the award program, beams when you ask her for examples. Among her favorites are the two customer-service people in the Florida operations center who found a way to get money and a steamship booking to a woman stranded in a hotel in war-torn Beirut. Or she will tell you about the travel agents in Columbus, Georgia, who bailed a French tourist out of jail, the travel counselor in New York who drove through a blizzard to deliver food and blankets to travelers stranded at Kennedy Airport. Or the travel agent in Boston who managed to reunite a non-English-speaking Japanese mother, stranded in Boston because of a diverted flight, with her daughter in Philadelphia. The travel agent took the mother across town to the train station, bought her a ticket, and wrote out instructions to the conductor. Or the Mexican customer service reps who handled the circumstances surrounding the death of a client aboard a cruise ship. These services involved arranging to have someone look after the granddaughters of the deceased person until relatives could reach the scene.

As touching as these stories are for their purely human interest, they are also intriguing as examples of living corporate legends—"war stories" that illustrate and prove publicly that an organization does value and reward customer service. As Sathe puts it, such examples help everyone in the organization interpret and understand the values and beliefs of the organization. When the pivotal value of the culture is service, and the stories and legends of the organization revolve around that value, so do most other aspects of that corporate culture.

Let's consider a final note on American Express. If we take Gerstner's words and the hero stories in isolation, they can make the organization sound too good to be true. It sounds like a heaven on earth, an "everybody-is-so-nice" sort of company. American Express is anything but that. We know many people who have a bag full of stories about how tough the internal dealings are at Am Ex and how fierce the competition is for advancement to ever suggest that the company is a charity in disguise. But those who run American Express day to day understand that at the top of the list of the organization's considerable assets are the people who operate its thousand travel offices and worldwide communications network. In a sense the test of a service organization is the culture management creates and maintains.

EVERYBODY IS SERVING SOMEBODY

It is not too much of a stretch to say that everyone in a service organization has a service role, even those who never see the customers. This applies to administrative people—supervisors, middle managers, and even executives. Olle Stiwenius of Scandinavian Airlines asks, "What is the purpose of the organization?" And he answers his own question in this way, "*Support.* The organization exists to support the people who serve the customer. It has no other meaning, no other purpose."

It's one thing to get the frontline people into a customer-oriented mode. It's quite another to sell that gospel to people in noncontact roles. It often happens that inside people, those who never deal with the customer, become preoccupied with inside concerns. They may spend so much time and effort dealing with information, procedures, forms, and reports that they become completely introverted in their point of view. "It's somebody else's job to take care of the customer. My job is to make sure these reports get in on time."

When inside people lose the sense of being connected to the

customer, regardless of how distant the connection may be, they become bureaucrats. They can no longer see how the results they produce help the company meet the wants and needs of the market. It telegraphs a profound misconception when a person says, "I don't have anything to do with the customers."

The simple message to all of the people in a service organization is:

> IF YOU'RE NOT SERVING THE CUSTOMER,
> YOU'D BETTER BE SERVING SOMEONE WHO IS.

This is an important realization, and we believe it qualifies as a bona fide principle of service management.

At People Express Airlines the employees work hard at remembering who the customer is and what the customer wants and expects. One part of that effort is People's universal job rotation scheme. Pilots take a turn at baggage handling and counter people do in-flight service. Every frontline team is self-managed, with employees taking turns at being the team leader. So far as we know, however, baggage-handling people do not get to fly the airplanes.

We can classify the people in a service organization into only three categories, according to this point of view. The first category includes the *primary service people*—those who have direct, *planned* contact with the customer. The second category includes the *secondary service people,* who usually serve the customer unseen, but who do have *incidental* contact with customers. And the third category includes everybody else; these are the *service-support people.* In a hospital, for example, a primary service person might be the attendant who brings a tray of food to a patient. The secondary service person in this instance would be the person who prepares the food for the patient. A typical service-support person might be the supervisor of the food-service unit.

The last statement borders on heresy in the minds of traditionally minded, authoritarian managers. Is management itself a service? The service management viewpoint says yes. In a customer-driven culture management becomes a special form of service, subject to evaluation of its role and its effectiveness, just like other services. Peter Drucker, the elder statesman of management thinkers, once wisecracked, "Most of what we call management consists of making it difficult for people to get their work done."

The service management philosophy, expressed in terms of the interplay of services in an organization, is truly a new paradigm for most businesses. The idea that everybody in a service organization has a "customer" strikes many American managers as novel, and some as blasphemous. It points the way to a new model for excellence in terms of the total organization. A service organization can truly "turn on" when everybody, or almost everybody, can focus on knowing whom to serve, learning what the important needs are, and finding effective ways to meet those needs.

MOTIVATION AND COMMITMENT ARE FRAGILE

It is obvious to the most casual observer that business organizations vary remarkably in the overall "spirit" that exists among their employees. In some organizations there is a high energy level, a sense of accomplishment, and even a sense of excitement on the part of the performance-level people. In others there is a prevailing lassitude, a burned-out sense of detachment and indifference.

The service orientation is something most managers dearly love to see in employees, and they recognize it when they see it, but most of them haven't the faintest idea what causes it. Many managers who take pride in their problem-solving skills feel bewildered when presented with evidence of mediocrity or toxic performance at the frontline level. Many of them have very little idea what to do or where to begin to solve this problem.

The lamentations are familiar: "What's wrong with people these days?" "Why don't they realize that the customer is paying their salaries?" And here comes the topper: "You just can't find good people any more." But really there is nothing wrong with people these days. It's just that people tend to react to their environments. Motivation and commitment are fragile and circumstantial. As we have previously observed, when the moments of truth go unmanaged, the service level regresses to "average," which in a competitive environment means "mediocre." To have a high standard of service, it is necessary to create and maintain a *motivating environment* in which service people can find personal reasons for committing their energies to the benefit of the customer.

Many managers consider the psychological factors involved in employee motivation a bottomless mystery, but we have known as much as we need to know about motivation since the time of Alexander the Great. The human being is a wanting animal. People commit their energies to the extent that what they do brings them what they want. What they want may be psychological—a feeling, a status, or an experience. Or it may be material—greenbacks are an excellent form of feedback. In any case the job of management is to engineer a motivating environment.

J. Willard Marriott, Jr., chief executive of Marriott Hotels, suspects that treating people supportively is antithetical to the attitudes of many managers. "Let's admit it," he says. "In a lot of companies there is a hostile attitude. There are people who like to fire people. Some managers may not know it, but they have created a fear-oriented climate. They may call it 'productivity-oriented,' but if their people are afraid of them and tattle on one another, it's no good." How does Marriott see his role as chief executive? He doesn't hesitate or hedge: "My job," he says, "is to motivate them, teach them, help them, and care about them."

How can we tell when we have a motivating environment? How do we evaluate the psychological setting at the grass roots of the organization? There are four important variables, all of which we can measure through employee surveys, which give a fairly reliable picture of the psychological state of affairs.

The first is the overall *quality of work life,* as reported by people from their own individual points of view.[3] This includes factors like job satisfaction, job security, pay and benefits, opportunities for advancement, competent supervision, harmonious surroundings, and justice and fair play. A high level of perceived quality of work life will not necessarily guarantee high motivation, but a low level will almost certainly demotivate people.

The second important indication of a motivating environment is the overall *morale.* Again, high morale is usually a necessary indication, but not always a sufficient one, for high commitment. It is possible for service people to have low morale for any number of reasons and still do their jobs with a high level of commitment and creativity. Conversely, it is possible for them to have high morale and yet not give their best energies to the job. But in general the link between morale and commitment are fairly clear.

The third indication of a motivating environment is a prevailing *energy level,* measured largely in terms of a sense of individual wellness and psychological well-being. Energy level, as we use the term here, implies the opposite of *burnout.* Service people in various stages of burnout typically have low personal energy and find it difficult to get excited about any new venture.

The fourth indication is a general sense of *optimism*—a belief that there are new possibilities, new ways to do things, new levels to achieve. Optimism often goes together with morale and energy level, but not always.

If the leaders of the organization hope to foster high levels of motivation and commitment on the part of service people, the first task is to evaluate the present motivational environment. If the environment needs repair, the second task is to repair it. Until the environment is reasonably ready, there can be little hope of lasting improvement in the service level.

BRASS BANDS AND ARMBANDS DON'T WORK

It is tempting for some executives to resort to theatrical measures, in hopes of getting the frontline employees turned on, as a substitute for the more expensive and more challenging process of reengineering the motivational environment.

A fairly typical approach is for executives to hold a top-management retreat, unveil the new corporate "campaign," invent a catchy slogan, and send all the middle managers out into the countryside as evangelists of the new gospel. Typical elements of this theatrical approach include making video tapes of the chief executive expressing his commitment to customer service, putting up posters, passing out lapel buttons, and selecting the "employee of the month."

Unfortunately, without an infrastructure in place to carry out a concrete program, the show-biz approach typically fades away in a few months. In more extreme cases it falls flat in the face of employee cynicism. Some executives talk and act as if they believe employees never think about what's going on in the organization, and never discuss things with one another. Many senior employees have lived through one "theme of the month" after another, and have long since given up expecting top management to follow through on any major campaign or program.

The employees in one large organization developed a simple catchphrase to express their attitude toward years of unfulfilled management campaigns—"B.O.H.I.C.A." It's translation is: "Bend over—here it comes again!" In the face of this kind of cynicism on the part of mature working adults, it's no wonder that many executives approach the idea of an organizationwide campaign with apprehension.

Note please that we are not saying managers should be grave and stone-faced—the embodiment of the captains-of-industry portraits that still hang in far too many boardrooms. Quite the contrary. Skilled executives have often been great cheerleaders. Bill Marriott says, for example, "If you don't generate excitement, you don't generate much." Donald Burr, president of People Express Airlines is practically evangelical in the way he pumps up his employees.

Showing enthusiasm and excitement about the mission of the organization is one thing, but partaking in a shallow, superficial "whip-up-the-troops" campaign is quite another. Your employees are as quick to spot a con job as are your customers. Like golf, baseball, and tennis, it's the follow-through that makes the difference.

An even more grave mistake than launching an unsupported theatrical campaign inside the organization is launching a collateral advertising campaign in the marketplace. It makes little sense to brag to customers about committed employees and quality service before the message is true. Many executives are remarkably naive about the length of time needed to make a major change in the organization's culture.

An advertising campaign promising exceptional service launched by a company that offers only a mediocre level of service can backfire with double effect. Before the campaign customers simply consider the service mediocre and don't think much about it. Along comes an advertising campaign promising excellence, and suddenly the customers perceive the grotesque disparity between the promise and the reality. It would have been better not to advertise at all in such a case. Better yet would be to make real improvements in the service level and then advertise them.

What we call the "brass-bands-and-armbands approach" usually doesn't work without the presence of three critical components:

1. A clear, concrete message that conveys a particular service strategy which performance-level people can begin to act upon.

2. Significant *modelling* by managers, that is, demonstrating by their behavior that they intend to enforce and reward service-oriented actions on behalf of the customer.

3. An energetic follow-through process, in which management takes action to provide the necessary training and resources and to align the systems and procedures of the organization so as to make them support the new service philosophy and strategy.

SMILE TRAINING DOESN'T DO IT EITHER

Another common approach that many managers take in their search for better frontline performance is trying to teach employees to "have better attitudes." This has its own peculiar pitfalls. Attitudes seem to be very important, but they are also very hard to pin down.

The concept of an attitude becomes especially elusive when one tries to isolate it to a teachable definition. We can give plenty of examples of "good attitude" and "bad attitude," but can one teach a person to have a good attitude? We want frontline people to be customer-oriented, and we know this attitude when we see it, but we don't know how to describe it except by example. People who specialize in industrial training often wrestle with the question of attitudes. How can we teach a person to be friendly, for example?

The attitude-training approach usually involves training programs that focus on specific social techniques, such as eye contact, smiling, tone of voice, standards of dress, and the like. Many employees refer to this kind of training as "smile training," or "charm school." To make matters worse, the training might have been inflicted on them by a hypocritical manager whose own attitude about people could benefit from a transplant.

We readily own up to a distinct bias of our own here. If you really believe your employees need training in how to be civil, or that they don't know the Golden Rule applies in public contact jobs, perhaps you need to review your procedures for selection and hiring. What are they doing over there in Personnel—hiring chimpanzees? A case where an employee truly lacks the most rudimentary social skills is a selection problem, not a training problem. Smile training, of the type we have been discussing, speaks eloquently of how little regard some managers have for the native intelligence of their employees.

Certainly, frontline people need to know how to handle irate customers. They also need to know how much abuse you expect them to tolerate, how to calm a fevered brow, and how far to go in righting a wrong. They may even need to learn some psychological self-protection skills, but *not*, we contend, how to "smile" and be civil.

Frequently the organization can thwart the will to serve through contradictory systems. At one major airline with which we are familiar, senior management gets service-oriented with clockwork predictability. Every few months the chief executive officer gets up to his elbows in customer complaint letters, so he orders up a new batch of customer service training.

Each time he finds a new vendor or a new in-house manager who is willing to take yet another crack at improving customer relations. Out goes the directive again: "Send your people to the customer-service program!" And right on cue, the complaints trail off for the rest of the quarter. But the second week of the next quarter is when the audit people go out into the field and run stopwatch rallies on the frontline people.

"They are moving the lines too slowly," announces the operations auditor after a few hours of timing the ticket agents. And of course the station manager—the boss of the ticket agents— feels the heat. Heat, as we all know, runs downhill: "Knock off the small talk with customers. Get 'em moving!" Then the chief's in basket starts filling up with complaints again, and the cycle is ready to start all over.

Frontline training can play an important part in improving the service orientation, but only if the people who receive the training see it as worthwhile and helpful. Too often experienced employees find the proposition of smile training or attitude training insulting. Some of them may desperately need to improve their social skills, but if they don't think they do, then training will probably not help matters, especially when nothing else in the system changes.

HOW TO USE TRAINING AND DEVELOPMENT EFFECTIVELY

Properly used, training and development can have huge payoffs in service performance. It is not always possible to trace a direct dollars-and-cents relationship between training investment and profit, but the qualitative advantages are often easy to identify. Industrial training methods have now evolved to a fairly sophisticated level, and training programs can involve more than just sitting around listening to lectures. Techniques of job task analysis, competency modelling, and training needs assessment can produce well-designed training programs targeted to the needs of the organization.

The key to making training pay off is knowing what we want the trainees to be able to do when they have finished the program. An effective training process starts with a performance analysis.

We must analyze the various jobs to be done in serving the customer well, and then spell out the knowledge, attitudes, and skills required of the person doing the job.

Once we know what it takes to do a particular service job well, we can figure out the most cost-effective way to help people learn those capabilities. Here we have a wide variety of options. If the job knowledge and tasks are fairly simple, then on-the-job training may be all that is needed. More demanding jobs may require special training programs designed just for the needs of those positions.

It is also important to recognize that different people may have different learning needs. A seasoned service employee coming from another organization or industry will probably not benefit from an A-B-C–type training program designed for entry-level people just coming into the workforce from high school.

There is also a place in a good training plan for a certain amount of personal enrichment training. This is the method Scandinavian Airlines and British Airways have used especially well. Personal enrichment training deals with matters such as self-esteem, confidence, values clarification, interpersonal skills, stress management, and goal setting. The theory behind this kind of training is that helping people review their personal effectiveness and rekindle their energies will automatically pay off on the job. The belief is that persons who feel better about themselves, and who have a clearer perspective on life goals, personal skills, and rewards, will have more creative energy to put into the job.

Personal enrichment training is usually a more promising avenue than trying to teach people to have a "good attitude," which is the usual approach in smile training. Rather than focus on attitude, the training dwells on personal skills. This avoids the intellectual trap of trying to define attitudes for people in sterile behavioral terms.

This is not to say we should try to outlaw the discussion of attitudes in the training center, merely that we should focus on more concrete factors. We can approach the matter of attitude on the job by encouraging employees to strive for measurable results that show up in terms of customer feedback. If we get high marks on the customer's report card, we can conclude that the service people have the "right" attitudes. The contribution of training is to help them figure out the right actions and tactics in dealing with the customer.

Bill Marriott is a firm believer in the value of training frontline people, and the impact the front line has on the bottom line. There are over 140,000 employees in the various Marriott hotel and food service enterprises, which he describes simply as a "people business." "We are in the people business. From waiters to maids to truck drivers, our employees must be able to get along pleasantly with others all day long." He adds that, by one estimate, company employees make 6 million customer contacts per day— 6 million moments of truth.

In the Marriott company that important customer interface isn't left to chance. Last year Marriott spent more than $20 million on training. To reinforce the effects of the training, every employee gets a regular performance review and participates in a generous profit-sharing plan.

SELECTION: FINDING PEOPLE WHO ARE WILLING AND ABLE TO SERVE

Another important part of the formula for success in service is filling service jobs with people who can do them effectively. Aside from the level of job knowledge and skill, which can vary considerably, there are several key factors that make for success and effectiveness in dealing with customers.

For one thing, a service person needs to have at least an adequate level of maturity and *self-esteem*. It is very difficult for a person to be genuine and cordial toward a customer if that person is moody, depressed, or angry about his or her life and circumstances.

Second, the service person needs to have a fairly high degree of *social skill*. He or she needs to be reasonably articulate, aware of the normal rules for social context, and able to say and do what is necessary to establish rapport with a customer and maintain it.

And third, he or she needs to have a fairly high level of *tolerance for contact*. This means that he or she can engage in many successive episodes of short interaction without becoming psychologically overloaded or overstressed. Contact overload is a recognizable syndrome in frontline work, and some people are more susceptible to it than others. The effective service person needs to be able to withstand many contact episodes without becoming either robotic, detached, or unempathetic.

All three of these requirements add up to what some psychologists are calling "emotional labor." In emotional-labor jobs, the self is the instrument of action. The service person must deliberately involve his or her feelings in the situation. He or she may not particularly feel like being cordial and becoming a one-minute friend to the next customer who approaches, but that is indeed what frontline work entails.

Unfortunately, all three of these key characteristics are subjective and difficult to measure. Pencil-and-paper tests are out in most cases, at least in American industries, because of the possibility of discrimination and because they are extremely difficult to validate. There are ways to help well-qualified people into service jobs and to help unqualified people out of such jobs. However, these methods involve measurement and feedback of performance, rather than "social traits."

Personnel selection, placement, and "replacement" also present special difficulties in service industries, largely because of economics. With few exceptions, frontline jobs are typically minimum-wage positions that have relatively little career potential. Turnover rates of 50 percent and more are commonplace in many service companies. Because of the structure of such industries and because of prevailing customs about pay and advancement, a service job is not generally a highly prized position.

A company seeking to hire frontline people for low-pay positions will usually find an adequate supply of "warm bodies" applying, but applicants tend to be minimally qualified entry-level people. These include young people who have left high school early, recent high-school graduates, college students in need of part-time work, and older workers whose lack of education, job skill, or self-esteem have prevented them from building careers. Some of these people may take to service jobs beautifully and become excellent performers, but in general the beginning competence level is fairly minimal.

Here we come to a logical syllogism. *If* we want a high level of service quality *and* need certain kinds of people in service jobs, *but* cannot reliably measure the characteristics necessary to select them unfailingly, *then* we had better have a means for following up on their performance to find out where we made the right choices and where we went wrong. This is why a successful service organization needs a well-defined process for evaluating its performance at the front line.

THE IMPORTANCE OF PERFORMANCE MEASUREMENT AND FEEDBACK

A customer-oriented front line is definitely what we want. However, it is sometimes a challenging problem to form a clear image in the collective organizational mind about what it means to be customer-oriented. In some cases it is possible to develop standards for service performance fairly easily. In other cases it may involve quite a challenge.

We need to communicate the service strategy to frontline people in the first place, so they know what we want them to concentrate on. Then we need to let them know how they are doing. The weakest link in many service organizations is the lack of a "closed-loop" feedback process that gives correction signals to the people who are delivering the service on a day-to-day basis. In many cases, if not most, they are left with their own guesswork about how well they are fulfilling the service strategy.

The need to provide performance measurement and feedback to service people reminds us of the need for effective market research in the first place. If we don't know what evaluation factors the customer has on the report card, we don't know what actions on the part of the service people will get high grades. Consequently, we don't know what to tell them about the effectiveness of their contributions.

In a large West Coast city, for example, managers wanted to improve the service level in the area of permits and licenses. City executives directed subordinate managers and organization development staff people to "find ways to make that function 'customer-oriented.' The people coming in to apply for licenses and permits are *citizens* and *taxpayers*. We're not doing somebody a favor when we provide a permit to build an addition to a house, we're doing a service. We must treat them like customers, not like naughty children."

And yet, when the staff task force went to work on the problem, they ran headlong into an immediate dilemma: how to define "customer-oriented service?" Just about everyone could offer some "for-instances" and some horror stories they would like to keep from happening again, but the question turned out to be more complicated than it had appeared. Was smiling at the permit applicants proof of customer orientation? Was speed in processing their applications the primary factor? Was personal treatment more important than speed and efficiency?

The task force came to understand that they needed to find out what report card they were being rated with in the minds of their citizen-customers. Without such a model, how could they hope to instruct frontline people in better service? How could they hope to train new people in good service behavior, if the task force itself couldn't define it? This led to a program of customer research that identified the key needs and expectations of the permit applicants and formulated a set of service guidelines for people involved in the permit process. Then the city could begin to measure performance by periodically repeating the market research in miniature form, along with surveys and spot interviews.

Measurement and feedback, properly applied, tend to make the organization a *cybernetic* entity, i.e., one that responds adaptively to its environment. The frontline employees are more aware of what works and what doesn't, and they have a better sense of their effectiveness. Management also has a better picture of what's happening overall, and can use the measurement information to see how well the service strategy is working.

8

Dull Moments and Shining Moments

> There is no higher religion than human service. To work for the
> common good is the greatest creed.
> —*Albert Schweitzer*

We can learn a great deal about service by watching people who
do it well as well as those who do it poorly. What follows is a
collection of vignettes of service we find instructive, thought-pro-
voking, and even inspiring. We provide here a variety of "dull
moments"—mishandled moments of truth—and "shining moments"—moments of truth when human creativity and commitment have paid off.

We present first a series of dull moments. Each of them exem-
plifies in some way a failure of one or more of the three critical
elements of the service triangle. Either the service strategy was
faulty or nonexistent, the frontline people failed to come through
for the customer, or the service system got in the way. As you
read each of the following vignettes, picture the service triangle
in your mind and make your own diagnosis. Which component
or combination of components of the service triangle went wrong?

Similarly, as you read the shining moments that come after
the dull moments, identify the key component you believe made
the difference.

Dull Moment # 1

In the lobby of a large branch post office in a southern California
city, we noticed the following sign:

"Parcel Acceptance Policy: parcels bound with scotch or mask-
ing tape, string, or twine are not acceptable. Please use filament
tape. We do not supply wrapping materials." It is no coincidence

that the United Parcel Service office, located right next door to the post office, does a booming business.

Dull Moment # 2

Many years ago, the following story circulated widely. A man found a large bug in a box of a well-known, widely advertised breakfast cereal. He wrote an indignant letter to the headquarters of the food company that marketed the cereal. Within a matter of days, he received a profusely apologetic letter, signed by a vice president of the company. The letter assured him there would be a full investigation of the matter, and that the company was instituting special procedures to make sure that nothing like it would ever happen again. However, clipped to the letter, he also found an interoffice note sheet with the handwritten message: "George— send this crank the 'bug letter.'"

Dull Moment # 3

A business executive was having dinner one evening in a coffee shop in the basement of one of Manhattan's largest hotels. This particular eating establishment has had a reputation for years of being distinguished only by the convenience of its location. The service provided by the waitress was a notch below the establishment's customary mediocrity. As he walked up to the cashier's desk to pay for the meal, the business executive's eyebrows went up when he noticed that she had taken the liberty of adding a 15 percent tip to the price of his dinner check before totaling it. This seemed just a bit too helpful to the customer, especially since he had decided not to leave a tip at all.

Dull Moment # 4

A group of passengers sitting on a commuter airplane in Buffalo, New York, got a disappointing message at about 10 one evening. The airplane was parked at the departure gate, during a brief stopover on its trip from Washington, D.C., to Toronto. Just about the time the passengers began wondering aloud why they were so long overdue for take-off, a gruff voice crackled over the intercom: "Please gather up your belongings and deplane the aircraft. This aircraft has a mechanical problem. It won't be going to Toronto tonight. The gate attendant inside the terminal will tell you what flights are available to Toronto."

As 60 disgruntled passengers trooped into the terminal, the gate attendant used the public address system to remind them to get in line in front of the desk and be patient. She offered no sign of an apology or any acknowledgement of the inconvenience, just the matter-of-fact announcement that the next available flight on that airline's schedule would depart at 11:15 P.M.

One of the passengers loudly shared the fact that he had quickly called a competing airline and found that that airline's regularly scheduled flight had just left about two minutes ago. He offered the speculation that the gate attendants had delayed the announcement of the equipment problem until they were sure the passengers had no other flights from which to choose. There was a run on complaint forms and some loud discussion about service.

Dull Moment # 5

A telephone call to a hospital center in southern California triggered this recorded message: "Thank you for calling——Hospital. All of our lines are busy at the moment. Your call will be answered in the order in which it was received. Please have your ——Hospital membership card ready. If you wish to schedule an eye appointment, call (number) XXX–XXXX. If you wish to schedule a physical examination, call YYY–YYYY. If you wish to make an appointment with the family practice department, call ZZZ–ZZZZ. *If this is a life-threatening situation, call ABC–DEFG.*"

Dull Moment # 6

A customer looked over the menu in a restaurant and saw very few choices that seemed appealing. Suddenly she spotted an interesting option: a peanut butter and jelly sandwich. "Now that sounds like just the thing," she beamed. "I haven't had a good peanut butter and jelly sandwich in ages. That and a glass of milk will hit the spot." When she asked the waitress for the sandwich, she received the chilly reply: "Sorry—that's the children's section on the menu. You can't order that."

The customer asked, "I don't understand. Why does a person have to be a child to order that particular sandwich? That's really what I would like to have." When the waitress firmly refused to place the order, the customer asked to speak to the restaurant manager. He offered the same story. "I'm sorry, ma'am. We don't serve children's orders to adults." Angry and incredulous, she decided to have lunch somewhere else.

Dull Moment # 7

A lone customer walked into a restaurant on a busy evening and signed up for dinner. When his turn came, the hostess escorted him to the far reaches of the dining area, and seated him at a tiny table located right next to the kitchen door. The waitresses bustled past him for some time until he finally stopped one of them and asked to place an order. "Just a moment," she said, hurrying on her way. A few minutes later, a busboy came over and took his order.

The busboy brought the customer the food when it was ready, and never came back. After some time a waitress stopped at his table, briskly dashed off a check, totalled it, and dropped it next to his plate. She hurried off without a word. He didn't have to spend much time calculating the tip. He left wondering whether he was becoming marginally paranoid, or whether single people really do get inferior service in many situations.

Dull Moment # 8

The business traveller got off the airplane, collected her luggage, and called the hotel to verify her reservation. The desk clerk verified it and told her the hotel's van would be there in a few minutes to pick her up. She waited outside the terminal and the van arrived shortly. So far, so good. A gum-chewing, wise-cracking teenager jumped out of the van, grabbed her luggage, threw it into the back of the van, climbed back into the driver's seat, and shouted, "Jump in!" She got into the van, figured out how to close the door, and settled back for what turned out to be a wild ride.

The kid drove as if the accelerator pedal was stuck. He puffed furiously on a cigarette as he drove, pausing only to swear occasionally at other drivers. He also treated his passenger to his tastes in music, as he had the van's radio blaring at maximum volume, pouring out the finest of acid rock fare. Arriving at the hotel, he dragged her luggage into the lobby, dumped it by the check-in desk, and stood around conspicuously. When she failed to tip him, he slunk away with a wounded look.

Dull Moment # 9

The largest computer manufacturer in the world introduced its personal computer, the IBM PC. As a result of the company's long-term reputation for quality products and a multimultimillion dollar advertising campaign, the machine soon became the best-selling personal computer for business people. However, the computer had a curious and almost unbelievable design flaw. People who bought it were incredulous that the company which had pioneered computers and the famous Selectric typewriter could make a product with such an obvious handicap.

The design handicap was on the computer's keyboard. In order to keep the number of keys on the keyboard to a minimum, the designers had used certain keys for double duty. For example, the ten number keys, arranged in a calculator-style keypad on one end of the keyboard, doubled as cursor-control keys. When in the cursor mode, the keys caused the blinking cursor-spot to move up, down, to the left, and to the right, so that the user could type things at various places on the video screen. When in the number mode, the keys simply put numbers on the screen wherever the cursor already was. The user had to hit a certain "toggle" key to change the keys back and forth between their two different jobs.

The problem was that the designers had not provided a way for the user to tell, by looking at the keyboard, whether the keys were in the number mode or in the cursor mode at any one moment. The toggle key did not latch into any certain position, and there was no light or any other indicator to show the status of the keys. The user would expect to be typing numbers, only to see the cursor jumping around the screen. He would try to move the cursor to a different area of the screen, only to see numbers appearing on the screen, scrambling the values he had previously typed.

At the time of this writing, over two years after the computer came onto the market, this peculiar and extremely frustrating design flaw still exists, as IBM PCs roll off the production line at the rate of one every 15 seconds.

Dull Moment # 10

At New York's Kennedy International Airport, a group of black African travelers, dressed in their traditional clothing, got off their airplane and walked into the customs inspection hall. There were several families among them, including small children. Judging by their answers to the questions asked by the customs inspectors, their command of English was rather limited. They seemed particularly confused by the hustle-bustle of the large crowd of passengers and unsure of the procedures they were supposed to follow.

After one family had gathered up its children and assembled its belongings, it moved toward the exit door. One of the men held in his hand a paper, which he had received from the flight attendant on the airplane. The African had filled it out and seemed to understand that he was supposed to surrender it to the customs official at the exit. As he handed it to the customs man, the official refused it and barked out, in the crudest of crude Brooklyn accents, "Go back and get anotha deck!"

The visitor looked baffled. "Excuse me . . . ," he stammered. The customs representative waved him off impatiently, and continued collecting declaration forms from the other passengers. When the African approached him again with a questioning look, this Federal ambassador of goodwill barked: "A deck! A deck! Ya need anotha deck! Ya only got one, and ya gotta have two!"

Finally an American passenger who knew the system explained to the visitor, in simplified English, that the customs representative wanted him to go back to the inspection counter, get another declaration form, and fill it out. Several bystanders expressed disappointment that this had to be the visitor's first experience of American hospitality.

And now for some shining moments. Here are some vignettes that show what is possible when people and systems come together to give their best.

Shining Moment # 1

One of the gate crews participating in British Airways's Customer First program got together with some of the flight attendants to discuss the matter of taking care of unaccompanied minors. The airline has certain legal liabilities in such cases, and they wanted to make sure the "hand-off" from gate crew to flight crew went properly. They quickly zeroed in on the term *unaccompanied minor* and asked, "Why can't we call them something more positive and less 'legal' sounding?" They came up with the term *Young Flyer*. This quickly led to the idea of treating Young Flyers as a special category of passengers, not as just legal liabilities.

The group worked out a Young Flyers program, complete with special ticket envelopes, a special boarding area for the children, and a special program of activities for them on board the airplane. The team, and British Airways, converted a liability into a marketing opportunity. The message was not lost on the parents of Young Flyers: British Airways takes good care of your children.

Shining Moment # 2

At a certain hospital in Memphis, when you arrive at the front door of the building to check in for your surgery, a doorman meets you at your car. He takes your overnight bag and escorts you to a special desk in the lobby. A bellman takes you, your visitors, and your belongings up to a preassigned room and helps you get properly situated.

When you are settled in, the patient-records representative visits you in your room and fills out the necessary admission forms. The hospital has adopted a "hotel" model for its layout and logistical procedures. Staff people prefer to use the term *guest* rather than *patient.* They try to provide as many of the features of a pleasant hotel stay as possible.

Shining Moment # 3

The waitress in a small coffee shop in downtown Denver is locally famous for her constant good humor and tireless attention to customer satisfaction. She bustles around the establishment, tending to countless details even when the place is packed and she is the only waitress on duty. One of our colleagues shook his head in wonderment one day as she showed how far she was willing to go for a customer. One of the patrons, a woman with three small children, was having trouble with the youngest of them, a noisy and colicky baby. The woman was feeling rather poorly herself, and was finding the children a bit too much to handle.

The waitress simply picked up the tot, coddled and pacified him for a few minutes, and proceeded on her rounds, waiting on tables with the baby perched on her hip. After a while the youngster calmed down, and she returned him to his mother for a nap.

Shining Moment # 4

A flight attendant on a Western Airlines flight decided to add some life to the standard, dull, robotic procedural announcements he had to make before take-off. He had the passengers in stitches with his commentary, which he delivered in a mock version of the same monotone voice that most flight attendants typically use.

"Ladies and gentlemen," he crooned, "there may be 50 ways to leave your lover, but there are only 9 ways to leave this airplane. Please look around and pick out the exit you plan to use if things don't go as planned." He followed with, "And now, please return your seat backs to their original, up-right, and most uncomfortable position for takeoff." To wind up his preflight announcements he said, "And if there is anything at all that we can do to make your flight more enjoyable, please don't hesitate to ask any of the female flight attendants on board."

After the plane had landed and was taxiing toward the terminal, he came on the PA system again. "Ladies and gentlemen, we wouldn't want any of you to reach the terminal building before the airplane does, so please stay in your seats with your seat belts fastened until the captain gives us the signal that it's OK to get up." His commentary earned applause from the passengers, both at takeoff and on landing.

Shining Moment # 5

One of our colleagues, while traveling in Japan, walked out of his hotel one evening, looking for a certain restaurant. He lost his way, and stopped into one of the many storefront police posts in the town of Sendai. One of the young Japanese police officers made a routine request for his passport, which the American had inadvertently left behind in the hotel. Since foreigners in Japan are required to have their passports available at all times, this was a rather serious matter. After the two local officers tried to question him in their broken English with little success, one of them escorted him to the hotel to retrieve the passport for verification.

On the way back to the hotel, our colleague's Japanese got better and the policeman's English improved, with the result that they found much to talk about. Our friend said that he liked Japan very much. The policeman noted that he planned to visit America some day. After verifying the passport, the police officer remembered the original purpose of our friend's visit to the police post. He escorted him quite some distance out of his own way to the restaurant, took him inside, turned him over to the restaurant manager, shook hands warmly, and went on his way.

Shining Moment # 6

An angry customer stood at the lost-luggage counter, berating the airline representative about the loss of his suitcase. The baggage rep had taken his report, filled out the tracer form, and apologized on behalf of the airline several times. The customer just wouldn't be pacified. He went on and on. "Where is my suitcase?" he demanded. "I'm sorry, sir. I don't know exactly where it is at this instant, but believe me, we'll locate it and get it to you as soon as we possibly can."

"I want to know where my suitcase is!" the man repeated. After several rounds of this process, the situation began to take on a bizarre, almost comical character. The other passengers waiting in line began to snicker at the man's peculiar behavior, his repeated question about the whereabouts of his suitcase, and his unwillingness to accept the reality of the situation.

Finally the baggage rep, who had gotten nowhere with courteous answers, decided to end the encounter with a comic maneuver. He held up his hand for silence and said, "Sir—look over there. Right there, on the floor. Watch carefully." With a theatrical flair and a magicianlike pointing gesture, he exclaimed, "Poof! There's your suitcase!"

The customer stared at the indicated spot on the floor with a bewildered expression on his face. He looked at the baggage rep, and again at the floor. The joke began to sink in, and as he finally grasped the absurdity of the situation, he began to laugh. The small knot of people gathered around the service counter joined in, and within seconds the scene was one of uproarious laughter. The man apologized for his outburst, thanked the baggage rep for his efforts, and went on his way.

Shining Moment # 7

An unconventional university in San Diego caters to working adults. This private institution offers degree programs based on an intensive schedule of evening study that involves taking one course at a time and finishing it in two months. At this school the student only sees the administrators once—at the very start of his or her program.

The student goes into the registrar's office and signs up for the entire degree program with one application. He or she receives a complete course plan and schedule, complete with beginning and ending dates, instructor names, book lists, and the like. This becomes his or her degree plan for the entire program. There is no standing in line to register for courses at the beginning of each term.

Shining Moment # 8

At a small college in northern Florida, a new extension director decided that the extension program should cater to the needs of busy professional people right from the start. He set up a one-stop method for signing up for courses, creating a support system that helped students with the logistics of their programs. Staff members in the extension office handled all the registration paperwork for the students, provided them with appropriate course outlines, and in many cases even gathered the textbooks needed for their classes.

In short, the staff members treated their prospective students like customers, which is what they were. Business people take evening courses of their free will, not because they have to chase degrees. The result was that enrollments more than doubled in less than a year, and the extension program earned the reputation of being truly geared to the needs of the business sector.

Shining Moment # 9

Karl Albrecht was staying in a small hotel in Sydney, Australia, recently, and needed to extend his stay in his room until the evening of his departure so that he could have a last-minute meeting with the Australian representatives of his company. He asked the hotel manager for an extension, but the hotel was fully booked and they needed the room for incoming guests.

"It's extremely important that we have this meeting," Albrecht said. "Is there any provision you can make? Do you have a conference room of some sort that I can rent for a few hours?" The manager checked the facility and said, "Dr. Albrecht, I think we can accommodate you. We do have a nice conference room on the top floor, and I'd be pleased to have you use it at no charge." Albrecht's travel agent now recommends that hotel to most of her clients who plan to visit Sydney.

Shining Moment # 10

A man wrote a letter to a small hotel in a Midwest town he planned to visit on his vacation. "I would like very much to bring my dog with me," he wrote. "The dog is well-groomed and very well-behaved. Would you be willing to permit me to keep him in my room with me at night?"

An immediate reply came from the hotel owner, who said, "I've been operating this hotel for many years. In all that time, I've never had a dog steal towels, bed clothes, silverware, or pictures off the walls. I've never had to evict a dog in the middle of the night for being drunk and disorderly. And I've never had a dog run out on a hotel bill. Yes, indeed, your dog is welcome at my hotel. And if your dog will vouch for you, you're welcome to stay here, too."

9

Quality and Productivity: The Measurement and Action Imperatives

When it comes to service,
we haven't begun to take advantage
of the improvement possibilities.
—*Karl Albrecht/Ron Zemke*

Though there are many issues to address in the management of service delivery, quality and productivity are at the core of most of them. Whether service is your primary product or only a part of it, delivery must be effective, efficient, and dependable if it is to have value to the customer. The service must be predictable and uniform; the customer has to be able to depend on what it will look like in delivery, how long it will take to deliver, and what it will cost. A Big Mac is a Big Mac is a Big Mac. It is the same, dependable Big Mac whether it is cooked, wrapped, and sold in San Francisco or St. Moritz, Switzerland. How you feel about the Big Mac is irrelevant. The McDonald's system insures that wherever you are in the world, when a "Big Mac attack" strikes you, you will be getting exactly what you anticipated; your expectations will be met. That doesn't mean that McDonald's Corporation is a 100 percent unwavering, "any-color-you-want-as-long-as-it's-black" production line. There are local market variations and adaptations, like the availability of wine in France and of vinegar as a condiment option in Canada and England. The folks at McDonald's world headquarters in Oak Brook, Illinois don't flinch when they are accused of industrializing the hamburger. Quite rightly they take pride in a Big Mac being a Big Mac being . . . —you get the picture!

Though McDonald's Corporation is an obvious example, it isn't alone in its quest for uniformity and quality in services, nor is it alone in achieving that goal. Caterpillar Tractor and IBM also make the delivery of service a quality affair, regardless of where in the world that service is delivered. One of the most chronicled of service deliverers is Rolls Royce. The following account, while undoubtedly apocryphal, has the feel of the obsession for quality that pervades Rolls Royce and the service reputation it enjoys:

> A member of the English peerage, the Earl of Puffnstuff, is vacationing in the Swiss Alps. On a winding road just outside the village of Zernez, his Rolls coughs to a stop. The earl and his chauffeur hoof it into the village, whereupon the chauffeur calls London direct to report that not only is the master's Rolls stopped dead in its tracks on a lonely mountain trek, but it also appears to have a blown head gasket. The driver is instructed to return to the car, and set out several flares; help is on the way. Sure enough, within the hour a helicopter bearing two technicians sets down in a nearby field. With a minimum of discussion the lads in spotless white coveralls set about their task. In less than 90 minutes his lordship's Rolls is again purring like the proverbial English tabby!
>
> Several months go by, and the chauffeur realizes that he has yet to be billed for the work on the Rolls. Thinking the cost of the helicopter alone will break his maintenance budget, he doesn't press the matter. Finally, after eight months and no invoice for the shock-troops service treatment, he phones up the factory service center. A cordial voice on the other end of the line listens to the tale and asks the chauffeur to hold while he checks his records. "No," the service manager replies when he returns, "there is no record of such an emergency service call," and after a short silence, "but of course why would there be? A Rolls Royce never breaks down in the field."

While stories like this enshrine the exemplary service providers, they also do a disservice. They inadvertently convey the notion that there is something mystical, or at least something superhuman, about the delivery of quality service. Such stories of service heroics suggest that the delivery of service, unlike the production of widgets, cannot be a predictable, controlled, and dependable process.

The myth of service quality as an issue beyond management control is so pervasive that when good service is standard issue for an organization, we go to great lengths to discount it rather than to learn from it. For several years Ron Zemke consulted in and around the theme park industry. After a while he realized that it was not just the Disney people who could create quality service.

It is absolutely true that Disney both invented the theme park industry and set the standards of acceptable customer service by which we judge all the other 500 odd theme parks in the United States. All the same, it is not true—as some people have wrongly implied—that only Disney knows how to meet those standards. Indeed, it is remarkable to see time and time again how well the management of parks like Six Flags, Opryland, Great Adventures, Busch Gardens, King's Island, and Caro Winds have recreated a Disneylike service environment while still maintaining their own unique entertainment identities. It is a fact, of course, that the management teams of many of these other successful parks are usually peppered with Disney alums. This tells us two things: (1) the Disney people do a great job of training managers; and (2) the act of creating a high-quality service environment is a transportable event.

During this period Zemke worked closely with another consulting group on a theme park project that—in his opinion—illustrated just how the feat of creating high-quality service management was accomplished.[1] His team gathered data, conducted studies, and eventually made a classy little twenty-minute videotape to tell the story. An interesting thing happened. Almost every time he showed the video to an audience of managers, he bumped up against the great "YesBut" phenomenon:

> Yes but that is a service business; yes but that is a unique situation; yes but that is the entertainment business; yes but their employees are all seasonal; yes but their employees are all kids; yes but that certainly would never work in our company—business—agency—industry. YesBut. . . .

Eventually Zemke simply stopped showing the video and telling the theme park tale to people. The point isn't just that people are resistant to change. People resist change as a part of their constitution. Or so it sometimes seems. The resistance this little service management video encountered was of a different sort. In this instance the villain was a strongly held myth about service: service can't be managed toward a predictable outcome because it is too people-dependent—too interpersonal.

Philip Crosby, the author of the Zero Defects theory, has encountered this same resistance to the notion that service production and quality can be managed and controlled:

The real problem comes about because the perception exists that it [service] can't be accomplished to procedures and specifications. Therefore, [service people] have the privilege of being sloppy and wasteful if they want to be. Because of this mentality, the price of this nonconformance in these "service" operations is twice what it is in manufacturing.[2]

IMPROVING SERVICES THROUGH INDUSTRIALIZATION

As we have previously mentioned, some service management experts have made disparaging comments about the approach to service on the part of McDonald's Corporation, K mart Corp., and Midas Mufflers. And while it is true that a McDonald's isn't a Windows On The World, a K mart store isn't a Tiffany's, and the neighborhood Midas shop isn't staffed by British Leyland's factory pit crew; none save these few effete critics, are suggesting that they should be. It is, we suggest, a touch of Yuppie uppishness that allows such critics to both decry and devour industrialized fast food from different sides of the same mouth.

Harvard's Theodore Levitt, a vocal defender of industrialized approaches to service, is steadfast in his belief that improvement in quality and productivity in the service sector is hampered by the erroneous belief that improvement in service is limited by our ability to change the skills and attitudes of the people who perform the service:

> This humanistic conception of service diverts us from seeking alternatives to the use of people, especially to large, organized groups of people. It does not allow us to reach out for new solutions and new definitions. It obstructs us from redesigning the tasks themselves; from creating new tools, processes, and organizations; and, perhaps, even from eliminating the conditions that created the problems.[3]

Levitt's point is not that all services should be automated, or that the people providing them should be turned into mindless semiautomatons. Far from it! His point is that when it comes to service, we haven't begun to take advantage of the improvement possibilities of automation. To Levitt, the fact that the MacDonald's approach achieves "the carefully controlled execution of each outlet's central function—the rapid delivery of a uniform, high-quality mix of prepared foods in an environment of obvious cleanliness, order, and cheerful courtesy," on a nationwide basis—makes McDonald's a wonder to behold and a marvel worth our study, if not our emulation. It's a fact that McDonald's has become a runaway commercial success as the result of a system that emphasizes the substitution of equipment for people wherever possible as well as the setting of explicit performance standards and methods for people to observe. All this simply suggests that we have barely begun to understand what possibilities there are for improving both the productivity and quality of service.

Levitt is also quick to point out that fast food is not the only service domain where industrialization has been beneficial. The mutual fund is a way of getting people to invest in the stock market without the expense of multiple sales calls and transactions. Expertise is concentrated in the fund managers, thus sparing customers and salespeople the need to duplicate needlessly that same expertise. The bank credit card—Mastercard, Visa, and so forth—is a simple way of extending loans to reliable bank customers without the expense of rechecking their creditworthiness every time they need to have credit. And finally, let's consider the humble supermarket. The substitution of self-service for clerk service has helped contain food prices, speed up the food shopping process, and increase food shopping options for consumers. When industrialization of service works well and helps us as consumers, it seems eminently reasonable and sensible. It is only when we are contemplating the industrialization of our own line of work or our own business that it seems threatening and risky.

Service can be industrialized in three ways: (1) by using hard technologies as a substitute for personal contact and human effort; (2) by improving work methods in a systematic manner (referred to as the use of soft technology); and (3) by combining those two methods. In other words, industrialization simply means that you automate where you can; you systematize and standardize where you can't; and you stop thinking that some services are exempt from this formula.

The soft technology solution—which Levitt describes as "the substitution of organized preplanned systems for individual service operatives"—is the solution followed by McDonald's, Kentucky Fried Chicken, Pizza Hut, and Ponderosa Steak House. We have already discussed this approach. It is instructive to think for a moment of all the places where the soft technology approach works so well that we simply take it for granted today. The supermarket has been with us since the early 1900s when the Hartford's—the founders of the Atlantic & Pacific Tea Company (A & P)—began slugging it out with all comers to see who could make the most money by charging customers the least. The open stack library—can you remember any other kind?—was a service innovation of the soft technology kind. The Christmas Club, the mutual fund, the restaurant salad bar, the IRA, the packaged travel tour, and H & R Block, Inc. are all soft technology service innovations we take so much for granted that their basic design is invisible to us.

Perhaps the hard technologies are the service innovations we notice the most. The ubiquitous ATM (Automatic Teller Machine) the banks are struggling to establish as their major consumer interface is an obvious instance. Less obvious are the airport X-ray machine that has replaced the labor-intensive luggage hand search, the automatic car wash that has replaced hours of handwork, and the coin-operated devices, including everything from food dispensers to highway toll collectors, which are labor-replacing hard technologies. In health care, automation has improved both quality and efficiency. The electrocardiogram has replaced the physician's sometimes fallible ear, and automated lab equipment has taken the error out of the lab technician's hands. The home video system has replaced the old home movie outfit and cut out the expense of the finishing lab. In the home there are more mechanical service providers—washers, dryers, vacuums—providing more amenities than most of us could ever afford if we had to hire individuals to perform them.

In the realm of mixed systems, a good example are the Midas Muffler shops owned by IC Industries, Inc. These limited service outlets move the consumer in and out in a flash by using special tools designed for one task—removing old and installing new automobile mufflers—and by standardizing work procedures. The increasing use of WATS lines instead of airlines for sales calls is an effort to automate and standardize, thereby decreasing the high cost of face-to-face selling—estimated at $160 per call by McGraw-Hill Research. Transamerica Title Insurance Company has systematized and automated a service—property title search—that was formerly performed reliably by hand and only by a specially trained expert.

Citicorp, one of the driving forces in the ATM movement, is also a leader in the effort to balance hard and soft technology in the customer's favor. In a classic example of the struggle between processing costs and customer satisfaction, which was reported in the *Harvard Business Review* in 1979, bank operations experts spent six years unsnarling a foreign letters of credit system that at one point had accumulated a backlog of 36,000 customer inquiries and the worst customer satisfaction rating in the industry.[4] Applying both industrial engineering and advanced computerization techniques to the problem, a 30-step process was cut by two thirds, while both customer and employee satisfaction ratings steadily improved.

The point of service industrialization—whether hard *or* soft technologies are being applied—is to make more services available and affordable to more people. The principles of automation and standardization are a way to cut through the mystique surrounding many practices associated with services. The automation and standardization effort strives to make rational much of the illogical service that is still practiced today. A perfect example is medicine. Today there is a swirl of controversy around the artificial heart and the use of mechanical means to sustain life. This debate is a moot testimony to the achievements of service industrialization—and to the quandary such success can bring about.

THE EMPLOYEE-CENTERED APPROACH

A second approach to the improvement of quality and productivity in service is, while not diametrically opposed to the industrialization approach, quite different in look and feel. Advocates of the "employee-centered" approach speak of it as being beyond the mere act of automating what can be automated, and refer to its central thesis as "the intelligent use of human intelligence." Their favorite pastime seems to be conjuring up images of a service industry version of the old silent movie *Metropolis*, with service providers cast in the role of unthinking cogs in an oppressive, uncaring, machine-centered service system. Critics of the employee-centered approach see it as a surrender to the old myths equating service with servitude and a misplaced belief that advocating a labor-intensive view of work is the only way to ensure enough jobs for people in the future. Political and philosophical passions aside, it is also an approach with much to commend it.

The employee-centered approach is related to the quality circle and total quality control approaches that have been coming into favor in manufacturing over the past five years. The central strategy is to push concern for quality and productivity improvement down the organization to the place where the most should be known about the causes and fixes of the problem: the front line. The belief is that those nearest to the work are in the best position to solve the problems. As demonstrated at SAS and British Airways, this can be a very effective approach. The Scandinavians aren't the only ones to have seized on this strategy.

In Japan the quality circle technique, which is a part of the total quality control (TQC) approach, has been applied successfully to service improvement by companies as diverse as Hotel Okura, Yaesu Book Center, and MK Taxi. It has helped solve problems of increasing consumer comfort, decreasing customer waiting time, and eliminating employee discourtesy. If you fear we are about to launch into a rehash of yesteryear's "Japan as Number One" diatribe, let's assure you that on the whole Japanese managers are only just beginning to catch on to the idea that service is an aspect of business in need of managing. But in those few Japanese organizations where service management *is* becoming an issue, the service improvement effort is decidedly employee-centered. In general, those efforts parallel closely the TQC efforts we have heard so much about with regard to the Japanese manufacturing effort.

It is interesting to note that there is a strong countervailing view in the Japanese management literature. Many managers and theorists are concerned that the TQC approach is not transportable to service management. This view seems to revolve around three beliefs: (1) service does not lend itself to standardization and hence to control; (2) service quality is difficult to measure objectively; and (3) service employees tend to worry about trivial things, that is, they have a tendency to focus on solving the wrong problems with their self-defined efforts. Sounds familiar, doesn't it?

The first step in a Japanese service improvement program is "management by policy." Senior management formulates policy and strategy relative to the value of service to the organization and the need for service improvement. Middle management then proceeds to take up the issues of defining service, setting operational policy, and establishing the quantitative need for service improvement. The operational policy setting generally takes the form of encouraging employees to explore the causes of poor service and to take corrective action where possible. They are to focus their improvement efforts on the most important and pressing problems, and they are to set and attain a few select goals.

At the employee level, the improvement effort begins by training service employees to work as a unit rather than as individuals in order to improve their performance. Management in turn promises to heed employee suggestions and recommendations for improving service performance. Frequently the wage system is modified to reward increased service satisfaction efforts. All the efforts seem to emphasize pep-rally-like meetings where service employees are praised for their efforts and their collective determination to improve service.

There are two interesting and somewhat contradictory aspects to this training. On the one hand, there is an emphasis on small group problem-solving techniques. Employees learn to apply Pareto Analysis, Fishbone Diagraming, and other standard TQC techniques to the analysis and solution of service problems. On the other hand, considerable emphasis is placed on employees going beyond the manual and adapting to customer needs as they arise. In other words, there is a slightly schizophrenic tone to the TQC approach to service management at the employee level. The message is, "Let us find the best way to serve the customer and all do our job that way—unless, of course, the customer doesn't like it that way." This is a very difficult message to impart successfully.

In the United States there are a number of good examples of employee-centered service improvement systems that have much in common with these largely experimental Japanese programs. Honeywell Corporation, one of the big users of the TQC approach to manufacturing quality control in this country, has extended the effort to nonmanufacturing arenas. Quality circles and involvement programs exist in engineering, personnel, and technical publications efforts. A Honeywell subsidiary in the United Kingdom has been working with sales circles for several years. John Naisbitt reports that organizations as diverse as Inter-First Bank/Dallas, General Dynamics Corp., Standard Meat Company, and Miller Brewing have applied the TQC approach to service improvement. Service-focused quality circles have been reported in such unlikely places as the Veteran's Medical Center in Albany, New York.

But quality circles and the TQC approach are not the only possible approaches to employee-focused service improvement efforts. Gainsharing, a formal method for sharing the financial benefits of service improvement with employees—which also has a strong employee participation feature—has many advocates. Self-supervision is another approach interesting to people in the so-called professional services segment. Self-supervision entails transferring to employees those functions traditionally reserved for management. Development of standards and evaluation criteria, scheduling of service delivery, tracking project progress, and so on are in the employee's hands in self-supervision. The employee, in effect, takes the role of an independent contractor working under the organization's name and staff services umbrella.

THE CORE ELEMENTS OF SERVICE QUALITY AND PRODUCTIVITY ASSURANCE

Whether the service quality and productivity assurance effort is employee-centered or technology-centered, it always includes four elements: involvement, measurement, reward, and follow-through.

Involvement

Involvement has a multitude of important meanings. First and foremost there is management awareness; this is what Philip Crosby calls "recognition by management that the [poor service quality] situation exists."[5]

Second is the matter of management commitment. Management must acknowledge and communicate the importance of service quality. The simple awareness and admission that service quality and productivity must be managed isn't enough, in and of itself, to start the ball rolling. A strong affirmation from management to the rank and file of the organization that the situation must change for the health and well-being of the organization is a must.

Third is management participation in deed as well as in word. John Simmons of the University of Massachusetts contends that one in three employee participation programs fails because employee involvement is viewed as a technique rather than a top-to-bottom way of organizational life. If management is excluded from the mandate to provide better service, no matter whether the approach is technology-centered or employee-centered, it is not likely to be viewed as serious.

This leads to the fourth and final sense of involvement—employee involvement. In the employee-centered approach this is usually not a problem—as long as all the employees in the organization or functional unit are involved. But it is just as important in a high-technology approach to service management. The employees' participation here is more subtle, but none the less important. Involving employees in the process of changing the technology insures that the employees will accept their role in relationship to the new technology, *and* that the new technology will be applied to the most important issues. The era of the systems analyst as the supreme expert who need not consult with the person doing the job, no matter how unsophisticated the job may be, is a thing of the past. The user is a fundamental and critical element in any new system. That importance is twice as great in a service management system.

Measurement

Measurement is imperative, but a caution must accompany any mention of this element. W. Edwards Demming, the dean of statistical quality control methodology, cautions that improving your ability to measure a problem never does much to solve it. Here is how Crosby colorfully paraphrases this view: "Getting weighed 10 times a day in different ways would not change the weight a bit." While we have seen many instances where measurement of productivity and quality—when simply displayed for all to see— *have* affected the attributes being measured, the act of measuring in and of itself accomplishes very little.

Determining what to measure is usually easier than determining how it should be measured. Usually, the what is more than obvious, or at least becomes obvious after a little serious consideration of possibilities. The what is always squarely related to the mission, goals, and objectives of the business. And almost always you have to deal with a subjective, customer-satisfaction element as well. The trickiest part is developing a measurement system that tracks both the desired organizational results and provides information that can have an impact on the performance of subgroups and individuals.

There is a simple process that helps determine what we want to measure. It begins by identifying the customer's moments of truth, which we talked about in Chapter 3. It goes on to use the concept of the business proposition to help place organizational significance on the many ways the customer and the organization come into contact.[6] The business proposition, which is the model of what the organization is trying to accomplish, involves a series of inferences about the relationship between customer experiences and organizational outcomes.

FIGURE 9–1 The Business Proposition

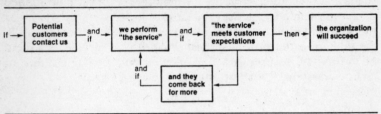

Figure 9–1 is a generalization of the business proposition of a service organization. It reads like this: "IF the target customer comes into contact with the organization, and IF the organization performs the promised service to specified standards, and IF the service meets the customer's expectations, THEN the organization has achieved its mission and will return a profit (or something else of value) to us." There are several inferences in the business proposition. The first is the obvious inference between customer satisfaction and profit. The second inference is between certain organizational performances and customer satisfaction. Finally, there is an assumption—an inference—that the service the organization wants to deliver is something the customer wants to receive.

Let's suppose that we dream up the following business proposition: "IF we can repair horse collars for an average of $7.50 a collar AND repair a single horse collar in 20 minutes, AND our customers like the way we do the work AND the way we treat them, THEN we will have satisfied customers, AND we will have repeat business AND we will make a handsome profit." The only way we will ever know if this oddball idea is viable, will be to: (1) figure out how to repair a horse collar in less than 20 minutes and at an average cost of $7.50; (2) determine what we have to do besides repair horse collars quickly and well to satisfy our customers; and (3) take the show out into the marketplace.

At the same time we must acknowledge that the idea will only get a fair shake in the marketplace if all the pieces are in place. If the model of what the business will look like and act like when it is running successfully is never brought into reality, we will never know how viable the idea is. Thus the elements of the model—the pieces of the business proposition—must be measured, monitored, and fooled with if we are going to have a chance at making a go at our horse collar repair business. Since our business proposition says we will win if we are cheap, quick, and charming, that idea dictates what we have to measure and monitor. We need to measure the speed of the work, the cost of the repairs, and the customer's subjective satisfaction with us and our work.

Here's a hint. Just as employees are a wealth of information about service improvement, they are also a good source of ideas about what should be measured. Crosby suggests determining the nature and method of measurement is the place where employee involvement begins: "However it is done [the measurement job], the people in the area know about it, they know how to do it, and they know how to count it. All you have to do is ask them to identify the correction method so it can be used to quantify measurement procedures."[7] We agree. Knowing what business you are in, that is, the business proposition, determining the moments of truth for your business, and asking the people who deliver the service to tell you what needs to be measured for them to know how well they are delivering the service—all these things are at the heart of a successful service management program. Without a map and a compass you can never know where you are going and whether you have arrived.

Information

Information is what management needs to control the business, and what employees need to know so that they can be sure they are doing what is expected of them. When we talk of information, we are referring to three distinct things. The first is an objective— a statement of what the individual (or unit) is supposed to achieve; the direction his, her, or the group's actions should take, and the amount and/or quality of work to be accomplished. The second is feedback or information that can be used by the individual or group to confirm or correct the direction, quality, and quantity of the effort. Finally, there is information about the performance— training in the knowledge and skills necessary to perform the job tasks in the first place. Without the flow of this information in the work unit, nothing much happens. People—collectively and individually—need to know how well they are providing the service they are expected to deliver if they are to have a chance at improving, or merely stabilizing, their performance of that service.

A lot of research has been done about the effect of feedback on performance. Working in a retail banking situation, Professor David A. Nadler has shown that by simply collecting information from customers and showing it to the employees of the branch, both employee attitudes and performance can be changed. Luckily it doesn't require a doctorate in industrial psychology to set up a usable feedback system.

Not too long ago Ron Zemke was reminded of that fact. He was standing in the drive-up lane of an automobile dealership, chatting with the manager of the service operation and waiting for the 10,000 mile checkup on his new Hupmobile to be completed. The conversation turned, pointedly, to the difficulty of having automobile service done on time. The service manager admitted that it was a hit or miss affair sometimes. Having nothing else to do but stand and wait, Zemke launched into an explanation of some performance feedback building work he had done for a General Motors dealership in Vancouver, B.C., several years earlier. He explained that as a part of an effort to improve the dealership's service reputation with customers, the service manager and shop mechanics had devised a system of keeping track of the percentage of on-time repairs. They even tracked the percentage of customers who said they were pleased with the work that had been done. (The service manager's secretary called service customers a day after the repair and quizzed them about their satisfaction.) On Zemke's next trip to the garage, the service manager made a point of taking him out into the repair shop to see two large wall charts that he and the mechanics had built of plywood and posterboard to display their current on-time repair standings and customer satisfaction ratings. These charts had been mounted on the wall of the lunchroom for all to see. "Is that about how those fellows in Canada were doing it?" the manager asked. "Yes, that's about it," Zemke confirmed without mentioning how much the manager had just saved in consulting fees.

A participant in a productivity improvement workshop we conducted a few years ago summed up an hour's lecture on performance improvement through feedback as well as the whole measurement and feedback dictum very nicely in about 25 words. "Let me see if I got all that," she said. "There are two things we have to do to begin to get better results: first, we have to have agreed-upon measurements for each department; second, we have to have a method of putting the measurements up where everybody can see 'em. That don't seem so tough." And the truth is, it isn't tough at all.

Reward

Reward, whether in the coin of the realm or the psyche of the recipient, is critical to a service improvement program and to a smoothly running service operation in general. While there is considerable research that shows the power of pay for performance, it becomes increasingly difficult to establish and maintain purely piecework systems. In service it is sometimes nearly impossible. Just the same, a service management must answer the question, "What's in it for me?" for the employees if the management hopes to promote a high level of service delivery. The success of employee-owned organizations like Peoples Express Airlines and United Parcel Service have not gone unnoticed. As a result, the concept of employee participation through ESOPs (employee stock ownership plans) receives serious consideration at compensation committee meetings these days. So do the more performance-based programs like gainsharing.

Money is an important and often overlooked part of the reward system of working for a living. If you don't think money is a motivator, just stop paying the people who work in your organization next Friday and see how many show up for work the following Monday. There are rewards beyond money that are important as well. Psychological gratifications ranging from happiness over a job well done to recognition by others that one is performing well are all reward possibilities. The rah-rah sales rally has been out of vogue for a decade or so in the United States, but has found a permanent place in the motivational tool kit of managers in Japan and western Europe. It also seems to be headed for a rebirth in this country as well. It has never been out in organizations with reputations for fierce employee loyalty such as IBM, Delta Air Lines Inc., and Hewlett-Packard Co.

What follows is a scene from the television version of a book entitled *In Search Of Excellence.* This work ties the whole matter of motivation up in a package available for anyone who wants to carry it away and use it. The scene takes place in the lunchroom of the North American Tool and Die Company in Oakland, California. North American, a small machine tool company, is short on technology but long on ingenuity. The company has, through employee participation, decreased reject rates from 5 percent to 0.1 percent, increased sales from $1.8 million to $7 million, and upped profits over 700 percent.

One of the keys to employee participation at North American

is owner Tom Malone's dedication to the idea that everyone who works for the company and who contributes to its success should be recognized and rewarded. In this portion of the video, Malone is handing out what he calls jokingly "The North American Tool and Die Refrigerator Award." The award is for a specific employee behavior he wants to encourage and reward. One day as Malone was walking through the plant, he noticed an employee running in and out of the company lunchroom, and carrying finished parts in and out of the lunchroom refrigerator. Malone quickly discovered that a number of parts being assembled for a customer order had been found too close to tolerance to be force-fitted. The employee, however, had figured out that if one part of the assembly was cooled in the freezer of the lunchroom refrigerator, the fit might work. And, in fact, it did. At the ceremony, Malone showered praise on the employee for his ingenuity and handed him a $50 check in appreciation of his effort.

There is an entire semester of applied psychology tied up in that little scene, but the wisdom can be distilled down to a simple principle: pay attention to the day-to-day successes and failures of people. Acknowledge and reward both effort and the accomplishment of important goals. This principle is the strongest motivational tool a manager can carry.

Follow-Through

Follow-through is a management commitment to make a service management effort not simply a program but a way of life. Almost any motivational program can stir people up and gain commitment and effort toward a specific improvement goal for 90 days. There are hundreds of highly profitable incentive motivation companies in the United States that have understood and taken advantage of this phenomenon. But isolated change and improvement programs tend to run their course, and then to run downhill toward the performance levels that existed before the program. The difference between a program and continuous commitment is management.

In successful service-conscious organizations, the demonstration of management commitment to quality of service is frequently embodied in the top person of the management team. When Bill Marriott wanders the basement of the Marriott Hotel in Washington, D.C., checking the cleanliness of stored dinner plates, he may be demonstrating more commitment to the details of service quality than some of his employees are comfortable with. But none of them can doubt that he cares about the quality of the experience guests have when they stay at a Marriott Hotel. When John Sculley, president of Apple Computer, takes a turn answering customer complaints as they come over the company's tollfree phone line, everyone at Apple Computer gets the message that customer satisfaction is important. And when Richard Rogers, president of Syntex Corp., makes a point of having breakfast in the employee cafeteria every morning so he can be available to employees who want to see him, no one doubts that he places a high value on employees' ideas and opinions. It may be, as some skeptics contend, that the Marriotts, and Sculleys, and Rogers would serve their companies and customers better by spending that time on matters of a higher order. But it is also true that their personal appearances have an impact on the beliefs and values of their employees that would be hard to achieve through memos, directives, or underlings.

10

Profiles In Service: Where Service Is an Obsession

> Quality service is a
> top down affair. It starts
> at the top or it doesn't start.
> —*Karl Albrecht/Ron Zemke*

For nine chapters we have pulpit thumped two distinct points. The first is that to achieve and maintain organizational success in the 1980s and 90s, it is imperative to become service-focused in your approach to the marketplace. Customers and consumers expect it, the necessity of developing meaningful competitive positioning demands it, and the profit and growth potential of services has never been greater. The second is that there exist examples of highly successful and respected service-conscious organizations from which you can learn to develop your service focus.

SOME ARE BORN GREAT . . . ALL OTHERS WORK LIKE HELL

Some of these exemplary service companies have never known any other driving force. They were literally imbued with a strong service focus by the founder or founders at Day One. They are the born great. Other organizations have come to a service obsession later in their histories. The difference between starting out as a service-conscious organization and learning the trick after the fact can be considerable. Conversion, it seems, is always a more difficult accomplishment than simply having a priori knowledge and faith. Ignatius Loyola's insight on twigs and trees is as apt for organizations as it is for individuals. Companies that have made that difficult transition have achieved greatness for themselves.

Last, but not least, are the companies that have had their service commitment thrust upon them. These include organizations that because of the nature of their business or because of the strong and obvious demands of their marketplace have learned to scramble—consciously or not—to serve and serve well their markets. There are lessons to be learned from all these companies, regardless of the route that has caused them to be distinguished from the rest of the pack by their success in running service-focused organizations.

In this chapter we will focus our attention on three companies. Two of them are by all measures successful service providers, while the third is making a difficult transition back toward service greatness. Aside from their preoccupation with service, the three firms couldn't be less alike. Each is in a different industry. They are very different in size, scope, and circumstance. And yet that one stroke of similarity—an obsession with service—makes them more alike operationally and spiritually than nonservice organizations in their home industries.

The first is Deluxe Check Printers, Inc., an organization founded in 1915 by W. R. Hotchkiss, a former country newspaper publisher with $300 in borrowed cash and a good credit rating. Several years earlier Hotchkiss had done an advertiser—a local bank—a favor and rush printed an order of bank checks on the newspaper's press. This order, followed by several more, led him to suspect there was a need for a business specializing in check printing—but not check printing the way every other vendor was doing it. Hotchkiss was convinced that the financial marketplace was ready for a specialized printing company that could quickly and dependably provide high-quality, accurate financial instruments.

In short, Hotchkiss's anthem was that a focus on providing *exceptional service* to the banking market—an act he defined as providing high-quality, accurately printed financial instruments quickly and in a dependable fashion—would win the day. It did, and still does. Along the way Deluxe has formed a unique and special relationship to its marketplace. That relationship is accurately reflected in the company's 1985 report to shareholders subtitled "Partnership," which stresses the theme that there is a significant difference between a partner and a printer.

The subject of our second case is British Airways. It is a rise-and-fall and rise-again story. BA, once the standard of innovation, service, and profitability to which all other European airlines compared themselves, arrived in the early 1980s somewhat the worse for wear.

Deregulation of international routes, abandonment of decades-old gentlemen's agreements among carriers, and competition from the enterprising and aggressive Freddie Lakers of the air transportation world had left British Airways among the rudderless. Unsure of the future of air travel regulations, uneasy about cost-cutting competitors, BA—like so many airlines—thrashed about on an indefinite course, unsure of exactly which heading would lead to stability and success.

In February 1983 BA chief executive Colin Marshall, taking a page from the Jan Carlzon route book, began the process of focusing the 37,000 employees of BA on the grail of *customer service*. In the process Marshall and his management team have been able to sidestep the marketing slogan trap and institute a strong, results-oriented program that places a premium on decentralized initiative, communication, and employee participation. Today that program is beginning to reap significant operational and productivity benefits. The emphasis in this case is upon the planning, effort, and involvement management must be willing to invest to become service-focused when the prevailing theme has been something quite different.

Our third and final case is CountryFair theme park, an upper-Midwest theme amusement park founded in 1979 by a young real estate developer who believed he had captured the essence of the Disney success formula. Evidently he was right. By 1982 his small regional organization had become so successful and profitable that when auditors from a large communication and entertainment empire looked at the park with an eye toward acquisition, they couldn't believe the books weren't cooked. The park had been built on time and within the parameters of the original construction budget, and had shown a profit from the day the gates were opened to the public. There was even an impressive cash reserve held for future expansion. Eventually the park was purchased, yielding the young entrepreneur and the original investors a handsome multiplier on their initial investment.

Three lessons are illustrated by this tale: the value and impact of the service concept, or formula, on long- and short-term planning, the value of the key impact variables concept on day-to-day operations, and the critical importance of employee involvement and job satisfaction on the success of a service-focused organization.

CASE I

Deluxe Check Printers: Service through Technology and People

In many ways Deluxe Check Printers, Inc., seems too good to be true. The firm was number 400 on *Fortune* magazine's 1983 list of the 500 largest U.S. corporations, up from 427th place the year before and 470th place in 1981. At the same time, it was 173d in net income, 15th in net income as a percent of sales, and 13th in net income as a percent of stockholders' equity. Deluxe has consistently been the dominant force in its market—the production and distribution of checks and other magnetic ink-encoded documents.

Forbes magazine recently estimated that Deluxe holds a 50 percent share of the check-printing market, making it three to four times larger than its nearest competitor. Chances are excellent that the checks in your checkbook were printed by Deluxe.

Since its founding in 1915, this St. Paul, Minnesota, based company has experienced only one money-losing year (in 1932, it lost $14,371), has never had to lay off an employee, and has had only five presidents—each of them homegrown within the Deluxe system.

The Buggy Whip Company with Laserlike Precision

In April 1984 *Fortune* magazine singled out 13 companies that for a decade had distinguished themselves in financial performance; their criteria—percent of return on shareholders' equity. This anointment of financial stardom was conferred on these 13 organizations because of an average return of at least 20 percent for the period 1973–84, and because they had never dropped below an ROE of 15 percent. Deluxe was number six on the roster—ahead of such acknowledged supercorporations as IBM, Maytag, The Coca-Cola Company, and Merck Sharp & Dohme—with a 1973–84 average ROE of 24.1 percent. Apparently surprised at the appearance of this low profile, low key corporation in such heady company, the *Fortune* staffer who wrote the accompanying commentary observed:

> Deluxe Check Printers [is] in some ways the wonder of the list. Through the decade, investors labeled Deluxe a buggy-whip company threatened with extinction by the "checkless society." Yet the company's sales quadrupled in the decade. They were boosted both by gains in orders that averaged close to 7 percent a year and by

price increases that customers accepted with equanimity no doubt in part because many do not have a clue what they pay for checks.[1]

Is Deluxe an anachronism—a three-toed sloth surviving among the tigers by virtue of its taste for carrion, for the leavings of a dying age? Is it as the writer suggested, a buggy whip company? Hardly. Eugene R. Olson, chairman of Deluxe, smiles when asked how his company can do so well manufacturing and selling such a simple commodity. "The first thing to understand," he suggests, "is that we aren't in a commodities business, we are in a service business." Olson is not, in fact, playing semantic Trivial Pursuit. He is expressing in simple declarative English the driving force of the organization: service.

That concept—the idea that providing fast, dependable printing services to the American commercial banking system would lead to the lion's share of what has become a $3 billion market for not only checks and deposit tickets but also for other forms and products as well—was exactly what the firm's founder W R. Hotchkiss had in mind in 1915. Fast, dependable service became a formalized, operational goal under the company's second president, George McSweeney, a marketing oriented individual who declared that fast service at Deluxe meant that all orders would be received, processed, printed, and shipped in a maximum turn-around of two days. The two-day goal became an assessable service standard under Deluxe's next CEO, Joseph L. Rose, an operations oriented gentleman who introduced systematic measurement into the system and focused much of his tenure on simplifying and standardizing the production process through the application of new technologies. By putting production competence into *machines* and *systems*, Deluxe has continually been able to keep people free to expedite, quality check, and troubleshoot. Operators who are freed of heavy craft responsibilities have brain time available for thinking of ways to improve current operations and for attending to the service aspects of the job. The result is a production capacity as errorfree and smoothly running as the vaunted Apple Macintosh facility in Cupertino, California.

Today, under the Olson regime, the concepts of service, quality, and dependability have been expanded to include every customer contact. One manifestation of that credo is that every proposed innovation in internal functioning must be examined not only in terms of its dollar and cents impact on the organization but also in terms of its impact on the customers and consumers as well. A proposed operations change that saves money but that inconveniences the customer or the consumer is more likely to be rejected than one favoring the customer but encumbering the corporation. Olson is insistent about the importance of service to the Deluxe success story. "It is the single most important reason for our growth and for customer confidence in us. Nothing we do is more important than looking after service."

The result of this obsession with service to the organization's customers (the commercial banks, S & Ls, credit unions, and investment houses) and to the consumer (the actual buyers and users of the checking products) is reflected in large and small decisions and operational processes. A small sampling is instructive.

Production. In order to keep to the two-day standard and minimize the time it takes for an order to reach the consumer after it has left the printing plant, production and distribution are kept as close to the customer as possible. The result is that Deluxe has 61 production plants coast to coast. The plants are regionally organized in a pattern roughly paralleling the nine U.S. federal banking districts. Each plant is run as a semi-independent business with P & L accountability and a business plan. A plant is not strictly free to do what it will in the entrepreneurial sense. Quality and timeliness standards are established and monitored closely by the corporate center. If a plant falls below the standard requiring 95 percent of received orders be through the production cycle in two days for more than a short period, or below 90 percent on any given day, inquiries are made as to the steps being taken to isolate and remedy the problem. Likewise, technological innovations are controlled from St. Paul, where production equipment is created, patented, and manufactured. (Many of the industry's key production innovations sport a Deluxe patent.)

A secondary consequence of the decentralization of production is the "feel" that pervades the organization. Although Deluxe has more than 10,000 employees, individual units have the feel of small companies. Likewise, the local units are not overburdened with directives from headquarters. Though all manufacturing machinery is developed and tested in an experimental operations facility near the corporate headquarters, the majority of new process ideas and production innovations come from people working in the 61 facilities and not from an esoteric "skunk works" filled with mad, semisocialized geniuses or from a white-coat, sterile R & D operation.

According to Frank Matschina, a 19-year Deluxe veteran and manager of the company's alternate methods plant—the facility where experimental methods and new procedures are tested under production conditions:

> What we do here at this plant is try out the ideas people in the 60 other plants come up with for improving production. They know they will be recognized for their ideas; they know that no one gets laid off for automation reasons, and that good ideas improve the profit sharing that everyone benefits from. So we don't have any contests or suggestion boxes. They aren't needed here.

Service.   At almost every conceivable contact point, service is measured and analyzed. In the customer service area, for instance, not only is transaction satisfaction measured but so are such critical process points as the average departmental "ring time"—the number of times the phone rings before it is answered. This simple measurement, first used by Emery Airfreight, is highly correlated to customer satisfaction with service personnel.

The service obsession is so pervasive that the annual report to shareholders contains not only the organization's dollars and cents record but its service record for the year as well. The 1983 report, for instance, reported that the accuracy rate for all manufacturing facilities was 99.1 percent and the two-day turnaround schedule met for 95.6 percent of all orders.

When we asked why these figures show up in a report to shareholders, Olson explained:

> It is the most important number in the report to the people who work inside Deluxe. They want to know how they have done the preceding year and we want them to know. For us to omit the service and accuracy figures, after all the emphasis we place on them in our day-to-day operation, would, and I think rightfully, lead our people to call into question whether we mean what we say about service. If our annual report was just for stock analysts we might think about leaving those numbers out. But to us, inside Deluxe, they are the most important numbers in the report.

Sales staff.   Deluxe salespeople, unlike most industrial salespeople, are salaried not commissioned. As Olson explains it, "The sales force is there to sell *and* service the customer. With a commissioned sales force customers never receive the attention they deserve. The temptation is to ignore customers unless they are being sold something or are complaining about problems. We don't think that is healthy for the organization or a very professional attitude toward the customer." An outcome of this position is that the sales force has traditionally been skilled at gathering intelligence about the changing needs of customers as well as servicing and selling, without suffering economically for it.

It is this freedom to stay close to customers—the result of sales people being freed from a commission-based salary system—that has over the years lead to product innovations such as stubless checks, personalized checks, distinctive colors, and scenic checks. It has put Deluxe in a position to influence federal standards for magnetic encoded checks and to anticipate and have the product ready when NOW accounts came along. When nontraditionals such as brokerage houses and retailers moved into the financial services business, Deluxe was neither surprised nor caught flatfooted. It had anticipated the need and had special products ready for the roll out.

Delivery. A few years ago it became apparent that it was taking longer for a completed order to reach a consumer through the mails than for Deluxe to produce it. Deluxe went to Congress and lobbied to have the U.S. postal regulations modified so that Deluxe and other so-called bank stationers could act as postal substations—thus taking on additional tasks for themselves—but speeding delivery of product to their customers' customers.

Lessons from Deluxe

When asked to share the secrets of building and maintaining a successful service-focused organization, Deluxe's chairman is refreshingly candid. "I don't know if I can do that. When managers—such as myself—have grown up in a culture that places such an emphasis on service, and that places such a premium on promotion from within, the service orientation is just a part of what gets passed along." This confirms again that it is hard to study the choreography when you are busy doing the dance.

Just the same, Olson's articulation of what for him seem critical factors in maintaining a strong service commitment are insightful and instructive. Below are listed the five observations he made and our commentaries on them.

The service commitment must be institutionalized to be effective. Chairman Olson stresses the involvement in service by stating: "It is important that everybody in the organization is involved in service. If only a few people at the top are thinking about it or concerned with it, there will be no service. Everyone has to be involved, everyone has to be concerned, and everyone [has to understand] . . . what service means and be committed to it."

There is a ring of relatedness here to Stanley M. Davis's discussion of the concept of guiding and daily beliefs, and the relationship of the cultural underpinnings to organizational strategy:

> Guiding beliefs are precepts upon which strategies get formulated, while daily beliefs affect whether strategies get implemented. When corporate culture is healthy, the daily beliefs flow from the guiding beliefs. They are translation and enactment of the basic tenets. The more unlinked the daily beliefs are to the guiding ones, the more unhealthy is the corporate environment.[2]

The understanding that the service concept must be stated sold, and sanctioned over and over until it becomes ingrained into the fabric of the organization is not to be underrated. Levinson and Rosenthal (in their book *CEO*) and Peters and Waterman (in *In Search Of Excellence*) emphasize the importance of the leader in setting the tone for the organization's culture and for developing commitment to his or her vision of the organization's goals. The hero stories and strong forging ahead accounts are as deeply rooted and important at Deluxe as they are at IBM.

Most emphatic—and most clear—about the impact of culture on organizational change, and the respect management must have for the impact of culture is this statement by Stanley M. Davis: "Culture, and therefore strategy, is a top-down affair. If the CEO ignores culture, he will be formulating strategy without its being grounded in what the company stands for, and he will be attempting to implement it without taking into account the major force for its success or failure."[3]

In line with this emphasis on management's responsibility to move the service message out into the organization to keep it alive, is Olson's response to our question about how strategy is set at Deluxe; "Oh we have a strategic planning person but he is a very practical person," to which was later added, "The strategic planning people and the financial people spend a lot of their time talking to—teaching—other managers about strategy and finance. The planning starts at the regional level so that is where the skills have to be." The idea of management—especially the CEO—as teacher and keeper of the corporate Rosetta stone is an especially strong theme, again, in the research of Levinson and Rosenthal and of Peters and Waterman.

In Olson's words,

Our (management's) job is to make it an idea they buy into, that they see as real, and that they share as important to the company and to their own growth. . . . When we go out and talk with people, we don't talk in generalities about productivity or about being profitable, we talk in concrete terms about good service and service goals, and how service keeps us competitive in the marketplace.

Service is a goal and a norm, but not a program. The idea of service as a program, or the focus of a program, seems repugnant at Deluxe. "We haven't a lot of special motivational programs or special incentives for good service here," Olson emphasized. The similarity with Carlzon's view that "if you are in a service business, then service is everyone's business," is obvious. Even though Deluxe has a large customer service unit, it is understood within the organization that the work of that unit is customer relations—communication, question answering, taking care of rush and special orders, looking into problems first, and the like—but the job of serving the customer is everyone's-job.

Be aware of, and anticipate the customers' needs. The "stay close to the customer" message has been turned into an aphorism of wall-plaque proportions by Peters and Waterman enthusiasts. And though it has become a hollow "Amen" in many organizations, it is far from being a tatted pillow sampler at Deluxe. It is a way of life for managers and public contact people alike.

It is also a tacit acknowledgment of the phenomenon of customer experiencing or maturation; the idea that the criteria customers judge your products and service by change as the customers become more experienced with your product and more sophisticated in general.[4] In Olson's words, "Our customers' needs keep changing, so we must be in the field looking at that all the time." When pressed for details, Olson describes a three-pronged approach to remaining sensitive and responsive to the market's needs:

We of course have a market research department that keeps track of our industry. And our sales people are in the field every day, talking to customers, getting information from customers on everything from their views on the number of checks and deposit slips that should be in a package to their use of EFT (electronic funds transfer). We also read the same [industry] literature our customers read and belong to the same associations.

As simple and straightforward as all this seems, we should be aware that execution is all. The Deluxe approach is unique. The Deluxe salesperson acts as a consultant to his or her clients. "Some of our customers pretty much know what they want from us, and what we are and aren't already providing them that they want us to look at. Others expect us to be more proactive and to have ideas to bounce off them."

Thus the customer is both source and sounding board for product and service innovation. But in addition to doing the usual market research things, Deluxe market research people apparently listen carefully to what they hear. The company has steadfastly refused to be panicked by the smoke and noise about the checkless society concept that has been a part of the banking industry's "Griswald predicts" literature for more than a decade. Though Deluxe has made a number of significant gestures away from total dependence on checks as their mainstay product, there is no sense of urgency, and certainly no panic, in their steps toward diversification. According to Olson:

> We follow the key indicators very closely. And we continually find EFT to account for a very small percentage of the over 45 billion banking transactions Americans make annually. In addition, our consumer research continues to tell us that [end users] are more interested in the security of transactions than anything else. They feel that, in a squabble over a payment, the paper check is still the best proof they can have of a transaction. Until the consumer stops being happy with checks, EFT will be in the slow growth stage.

Thus reassured by the marketplace, Deluxe continues the quest for better ways to penetrate and to serve a market it has long come to dominate, much to the consternation of *Forbes* magazine, which has twice forecast its demise, and not infrequently to the bemusement of the industry it serves.

Being active in the trade association community has paid off well for Deluxe several times in its history. In 1959, for example, when the American Banking Association released specifications for bank checks printed in magnetic ink—those odd little numbers running along the bottom of your personal and payroll checks— the specs were no surprise to anyone at Deluxe, since then president George McSweeney had been a key mover and shaker in the development of those standards.

Challenge yourself and your assumptions. As is the case for any organization that dominates its industry, the Number One threat to Deluxe is complacency. In Olson's words, "You have to look at yourself, to be introspective about yourself and your assumptions about the business you are in and where it is headed." Unlike the Chinese emperor of old who could station a servant behind the throne to whisper warnings in his ear to counter courtesan flattery, Deluxe management has to make an effort to go into the marketplace and look for criticism. As a result, Olson spends a significant amount of his time with customers, stockholders, and industry-knowledgeable people "asking them about our strengths and weaknesses."

In recent years Deluxe people have sensed some need to begin moving into product areas other than checks and check-related documents. They have moved experimentally, and with characteristic caution into the computer forms market and the direct mail sale of executive desk accessories ranging from preinked name and address stamps to pocket calculators. But even here, the traditional Deluxe service focus is the driving force. In the computer forms business Deluxe positions itself as the fast and accurate producer, offering a three-day turnaround on forms orders in an industry that traditionally measures response in weeks. When Olson expresses the Deluxe expansion and acquisition philosophy as "moving only into businesses tied to what we know how to do," the allusion isn't to a search for new places to put ink on paper, but for ways to serve a market faster and better than anyone else.

CASE II
British Airways: Relearning the Service Focus

In days of yore, when air travel was a dress-up affair, British Airways was a service legend. The same spit and polish that made a trip on a British liner a voyage made a flight on British Airways a shining adventure. Then came the nationalization of everything, and BA took on the dowdy aspects of just another poorly run public utility. For years the company was the quintessence of a stodgy government-owned company. It took a beating during the economic downturn of the early 1980s, as did most of the airline industry.

Seeing Scandinavian Airlines pull out of its economic nosedive with its much touted service management program, British Airways executives began to wonder whether the same medicine might not be good for their company. In February 1983 chief executive Colin Marshall undertook a major effort to upgrade the company's service image. Following a top-down strategy, his first step was to establish a task force to find ways to improve the level and consistency of the carrier's customer service.

Marshall gave the task force a modest objective: to find a way to make British Airways "the best airline in the world." He went one step further, identifying customer service as the all-important, Number One priority for the entire company. His charge to the task force left no room for doubt about the direction he wanted to take: "We are determined to be the best airline in the world. We must make quality of service paramount. This means putting the customer first in everything we do."

The task force proposed a comprehensive campaign to raise the standards of service in all operations of the company, not just in the air. In addition, as a part of that goal, the task force realized that dissatisfied employees tend to give unsatisfactory service. The task force's job was to find ways to foster a higher level of morale, motivation, and commitment among BA employees. Their first act was to commission an extensive market research effort aimed at getting a fix on the company's current public image.

The outcome of that effort has been discussed earlier. To recap, survey takers stopped hundreds of passengers in both Heathrow and Gatwick airports in England and asked them detailed questions about their flying experiences. They interviewed people who were familiar with BA and had flown the carrier frequently as well as travelers who had never flown with the airline. Their investigation focused on discovering critical incidents and experience factors that affect customer goodwill and that, when attended to properly, would offer opportunities for generating new business.

The four goodwill factors that came out of the market research gave the task force a clear picture of what passengers seemed to expect from an airline. The four factors of highest value were:

1. Care and concern on the part of public contact people.
2. Problem solving capability in frontline personnel.
3. Spontaneity or flexibility in the application of policies and procedures.

4. Recovery, or the ability of frontline people to make things right for the customer when they have somehow gone astray.

When this report card was handed in, British Airways did not fare exceptionally well. The message, in the main, was that BA was plain vanilla in the consumer's eyes—not much worse than other carriers, but certainly not any better. The task force could at least take solace in the fact that it now had a clear idea of what criteria consumers were using to judge them by.

Armed with this fresh customer preference data, the task force executed a four-part campaign intended to communicate the service-first message to every last person in the organization from London to Hong Kong. The first phase was an intensive two-day seminar for frontline people. The goals of this expensive seminar effort, which was mounted for BA by Time Manager International (the same seminar company SAS had employed), were to sell the results of the market research and to convey the message that BA was going to pull out the stops to meet those expectations.

The training sessions were designed loosely so as to involve employees from a wide diversity of disciplines, levels, and assignments within the company. The purpose was to bring a variety of viewpoints to the discussions of how *all* British Airways employees could contribute to improved customer service. A second part of the agenda was to put forward the notion that internal service— work done in the bowels of the business—was as important to customer service satisfaction as direct customer contact efforts. The sessions were, by American training standards, massive rallies, averaging 170 attendees per session.

Much of the content of these sessions focused on the personal development of the attendees. Topics were as personal as coping with the stress of customer contact, dealing with feelings generated by intensive customer service activities, and communicating effectively and assertively under pressure. It was not the usual fare of corporate training programs. The content of company-provided job training in both Europe and the United States runs much more to the operational aspects of doing a job. The hypothesis here was interesting. The conjecture was that by helping British Airways people deal more effectively with the personal issues it would ultimately make them more effective in their work.

The second cornerstone of the British Airways program was an adaptation of the quality circle approach to service improvement mentioned in Chapter 9. At BA the line level service improvement groups are designated "customer first teams." By November 1983 the first of these service improvement/service management teams was in place. Today there are over 40 customer first teams active in the United Kingdom, and more than 70 in place in other countries. By British Airways estimates, there are more than a thousand BA employees actively participating in customer first teams.

The idea behind the customer first team is to provide a forum for line people to develop and experiment with new approaches to service management right at the grass roots. One aspect of the responsibility given the teams is that when British Airways management contemplated the issue of developing new service standards, their decision was not to impose procedures and measures on a station from on high, but to give the matter over to the service first teams. To date, teams have generated several thousand service improvement suggestions. Suggestions range from extending office operating hours to better service travelers to revamping lost-and-found procedures. Recommendations and suggestions that have systemwide implications or that might require considerable capital outlay are bumped to the head office for review and approval.

Though a fairly new feature, the customer first teams have already proved sufficiently successful that the British Airways management has moved them out of the realm of experimental idea into the area of permanent fixtures. Donald Porter, manager of Customer Service Quality Assurance, publishes a periodic customer first team newsletter that is used to praise and communicate the teams' accomplishments. In Porter's words the teams have provided "an opportunity for all staff to be involved in the decision-making process necessary to get their ideas implemented."

The third part of the BA effort is a concept called the customer first workshop. Here, senior managers run workshops with their staff members in order to work out specific criteria for service quality at the front line. All across the organization, frontline people have developed specifications for their own performance. They gather periodically to examine selected aspects of the customer's experience and to study market research data pertaining to that experience. A typical service specification begins by explaining the customer's expectations for a particular service, such as baggage handling, telephone reservations, or food service aboard a plane. The second part of the specification describes what staff people must do to meet those expectations.

The fourth part of the program is the integration of service standards into regular frontline processes of training and performance appraisal. Staff members learn the various service standards they must meet, and they understand that their managers will evaluate their performance against those standards.

A key element of follow-through in the British Airways program we find appealing is the ongoing market research effort. Market research typically is a once-in-a-while affair. At British Airways market research acts as a continuous feedback system against which to measure progress. The surveying of customers, for instance, has become a routine and perpetual process. Interviewers gather data from over 10,000 people every quarter, and feed them back to Porter's office for processing and analysis. Unlike most management information, the flow doesn't stop there. The results are also fed into the workshops and back to the customer first teams.

Porter is particularly proud of his "quick-fire" report system:

> Whenever a customer makes a particularly emphatic remark to one of the interviewers, the interviewer is instructed to gently follow up on the remark and try to learn more about the person's experience. This will frequently uncover a report of some atrocity which should never have happened. The interviewer tries to get the customer's name, address, and phone number so somebody can follow up and set the matter straight.

> In such a case, the interviewer fills out a more extensive quick-fire report that comes straight to my desk. I read it and figure out which organizational unit is responsible. My objective is to have the report in the hands of the responsible manager within 24 hours of the interview.

In several cases, according to Porter, the quick-fire report has alerted managers to major incidents that could affect the goodwill of some of their larger corporate customers, who spend hundreds of thousands of pounds each year on air travel.

> By putting the incident in the hands of a responsible manager, we can get dramatic high-level action quickly. It makes quite an impression on a customer when a high-ranking manager rings up the customer within a day or two of the airport interview.

Is British Airways now the best airline in the world? That may be unknowable. But the customer first program has unquestionably produced some strong and visible signs of a new day for BA. We know that we have seen firsthand a marked change in the quality of interpersonal attention—warmth, friendliness, attentiveness, and so forth—exhibited in flight by British Airways employees. Our sample, of course, is small but it is an encouraging sign, nonetheless.

The mere fact that chief executive Marshall was willing to spend a small fortune training all 37,000 BA employees in the philosophy of the new approach is certainly testimony to the organization's seriousness of purpose. The follow-through has been effective, and the fact that the market research is being used as ongoing guidance shows BA's commitment to the learning process. The results from the customer first teams demonstrate a great deal of imagination and creativity.

Getting an organization the size of British Airways to move in a concerted way is certainly impressive, and the momentum shows every sign of continuing. We learned several tricks for our own work from their experiences. It will be interesting to revisit the BA project in the future—especially after the organization has been "privatized"—to see if the service management philosophy is alive and well and as enthusiastically embraced as it is right now.

CASE III
CountryFair Theme Park: Building Service from the Ground Up

Though all tinsel and glitter to the guest, a theme amusement park is a highly sophisticated, highly profitable, results-oriented business. Such parks are made all the more remarkable by the fact that, outside the Sun Belt, they operate only a few months out of a year, and are staffed primarily by 17- to 20-year-old students working for spending money or tuition.

CountryFair, a medium-sized, midwestern theme park, is a mixed attraction park. It has a mix of thrill rides, stage shows, game areas, and food service. Like most theme parks, CountryFair charges a fixed entry fee that entitles guests to free access to all rides, stage shows, and attractions. The running bottom-line indicator here, as in the industry as a whole, is gross dollar revenue divided by guest count, or "per cap" (short for per capita expenditure). It is a common goal to try to induce guests to spend an amount on food, gifts, and games equal to the fixed entrance fee. In marketing terms, theme parks—save the few giant, national monument-size operations—are essentially fixed-market service institutions, dependent on repeat business for their survival.

As a study in service management, CountryFair illustrates several key points. First, it is a stunning example of how powerful a well-conceived service package can be in the design and development of a ground-up service operation. Second, it demonstrates the utility of a competently designed and effectively utilized "measurement—feedback—reward" system. And finally, it gives testimony to the results that can be achieved when service employees are empowered to be flexible, creative problem solvers.

The Service Package

CountryFair was the brainchild of a young real estate entrepreneur (a publicity-shy type we'll simply refer to as Mike) whose total experience with theme parks, prior to the founding of CountryFair, had been as a paying guest. Like many of us, this young entrepreneur was impressed by the efficiency, smoothness of operation, and sense of delight he experienced on a family trip to Disneyland. Unlike most of us, he decided that it would be great fun to build a Disneyland of his own, back home.

That decision made, his approach to the business was far from impulsive. It was, if anything, quite scientific. First he spent a year visiting theme parks across the country and learning everything he could from managers and employees of those parks. He steeped himself in the dos and don'ts of the theme park business. Once his analysis convinced him that his idea was financially and managerially feasible, he struck out in the direction of developing both the physical and conceptual package that would replicate the success of other parks and cater to the uniqueness of his own native market.

His "business proposition"—our phrase not his—was unique and creative. On the basis of his observations of the industry, he reasoned:

> The purpose of a theme park is to provide a setting where people can have a large measure of good old-fashioned fun. If people have fun in the park, they will become both repeat customers and word-of-mouth advocates of it. This theme park will work when guests experience a *clean* entertainment environment, staffed by *friendly* people who provide good *service,* and find enjoyable the *show* (games, rides, entertainments, food, etc.) that the park and park people make

available to them. When all that happens, the guests will say they are having a fun experience.

These four factors—friendliness, cleanliness, service, and show—were, in effect, the organization's service package—the touchstones around which almost every operational decision was made. They were also the criteria against which all park performance could and should be measured.

The Measurement System

The four factors of the service package, when operationalized—that is, made concrete through experimentation and discussions with the management staff—served as the model, or reference point, in the development of a survey of guest satisfaction. The final survey was composed of 36 items designed to measure guest perceptions of the four factors—cleanliness, friendliness, service, and show—as well as items asking for guests' overall satisfaction with the CountryFair experience. After a little testing and tweaking, the survey proved to be a very sensitive instrument. It was useful in measuring both overall guest satisfaction and assessing the delivery of the four component factors.

Feedback of Results

Once the measurement method was locked in, the process of feeding those guest ratings of the park back to employees began. This was done in what we think of as a most unusual fashion, but one in keeping with the theme park culture.

John, the park personnel director and the program's biggest booster, turned a 50-foot-long by 10-foot-high wall next to the employee time clock into a giant graph for displaying "guest satisfaction" scores as measured by the survey. On this wall he charted a running average of guest ratings on each of the four factors as well as an overall guest satisfaction measure—the sum of the four factors. New survey results were added to the graph every other day. Scores from each of the 36 items were made available as well, but in a less spectacular fashion.

The meaning of the moving line on the giant graph was explained to the employees—who immediately dubbed the graph the "CountryFair Dow-Jones average"—and the individual survey items were discussed with the employees. The proposition that their treatment of guests, attention to their job assignments, and so forth, could affect the daily average became the focus of small group meetings between supervisors and employees.

The Reward System

Shortly after the feedback system was installed, an incentive merchandise program was introduced. The incentive motivation program was instituted as a way of recognizing and rewarding exceptional attention to customer satisfaction. Though the system was a bit complex, it worked roughly like this:

"Warm Fuzzies." Supervisors, and every 50th guest to enter the park, were given special tokens—small colored cards dubbed "warm fuzzies" by the employees—and asked to give one to any employee who made a special effort to make a guest's time in the park enjoyable. There was room on the token for guests to make a special note of exactly what it was the employee did that made him or her worthy of special recognition.

With a little practice and encouragement, supervisors became adept at using tokens, coupled with verbal praise, to recognize and reward good job performance. They became especially adept at rewarding good job performance on the part of employees with minimal public contact. As employees gained familiarity with the system, they asked for, and were allowed, the right to make awards to fellow employees and supervisors who, they felt, exhibited exemplary behavior.

Merchandise awards. The tokens had point values that could be accumulated and traded in for merchandise. The merchandise ranged from record albums and video games to 10-speed bikes and trips to faraway places, like Ft. Lauderdale, during spring break the following year.

Point value increase. After employees became familiar with the warm fuzzy program, a new twist was added; the point values of the tokens would be increased as the guest satisfaction ratings went up. In other words, tokens worth five merchandise points could never decrease in face value, but could as much as double in value if the exit survey rating of guest satisfaction increased far enough above the baseline. The employees immediately renamed the warm fuzzy tokens "CountryFair stock."

The fuzzy market. The tokens could be treated as the employees wished. Such tokens could be traded in immediately or kept in hopes that the Dow-Jones Average might rise. It was also possible to hoard, pool, buy, sell, trade them or to keep them as souvenirs. Each and every one of these behaviors, and several more, were often observed during the three years the program was in effect. (The token reward part of the program has been curtailed by the new owners of the park.)

Follow-Through

The measurement and reward program became an important part of employee small group meetings. Employees in the same areas of the park as well as employees in charge of the same rides, games, and food stands on different shifts would meet and discuss ways to increase the flow of traffic—and tokens—in their part of the park. They also considered ways to improve guest ratings so that the tokens those employees were holding might increase in value. Supervisors would use these same meetings to enlist employee help in solving particular operational problems or in addressing specific guest satisfaction issues.

In areas where particularly thorny problems might arise—cash drawers coming up short, merchandise inventory shrinkage, guest waiting lines increasing beyond tolerable limits, excessive trash accumulation, and so on—the park personnel director would intervene to the point that more formal problem-solving techniques were taught to the groups. It should be noted, by the way, that the small group meetings were never formally introduced, and attendance and membership were strictly voluntary. Groups were simply allowed to meet. The only concession to them came in the form of making meeting space available, and managers would attend a meeting if a group asked for their involvement.

Since CountryFair is primarily a summer employer and not a career opportunity for most employees, turnover tends to be high. It usually increases in August when employees begin to notice the summer slipping by and their friends' tans deepening. Park management took advantage of the existence of the feedback/reward/recognition system to do battle with the turnover tendency. Bonus points for days worked, for perfect attendance, for being on time, and a half dozen other "specials" went into effect as the season wore on. In fact, attendance control became such an obsession with management one season that an end-of-season drawing for significant awards (stereos, television sets, and an automobile) was held; eligibility was based on attendance. At one point employees had to be counselled not to volunteer too much overtime!

Beyond the gimmicks and special reward and recognition programs, the management of CountryFair made visibility and assistance an obsession. Back of the house (office-bound) managers were expected to take a turn around the park at regular intervals during the working day. In addition, desk-bound executives were regularly posted to the officer of the day roster, which included weekend duty. On particularly intemperate or busy days, managers frequently spelled line employees so they could enjoy extra work breaks. Managers and executives also had to be cautioned about too many hours in the park!

Where Else Can You Make a Living Playing?

It may be the nature of the business that causes such commitment to customers, fellow employees, and the enterprise as a whole. In how many other endeavors can the average normal Joe or Jane set out for the business world and end up with a little piece of show biz in his or her life? It is an industry that, when managed well, is rewarding and compelling. The attitude and the feel were summed up well by Mike when the sale became a real possibility and the closing date was almost at hand. "You know," he announced, "I suddenly realized this morning that this thing is going to go. And that bothered me. When am I ever going to have a chance to work so hard and have so much fun doing it again in my life?"

11

How to Teach an Elephant to Dance

Quality of service is now a top-management issue.
—*Karl Albrecht/Ron Zemke*

To recap what we have concluded so far: we live in a service economy and an increasingly service-conscious society. Service accounts for 60 percent of the gross national product and 70 percent of the jobs in the United States. Other developed countries are experiencing the same trends and patterns. Many more organizations are getting serious about the quality of the customer's experience, and more and more are finding ways to improve it.

Further, we have concluded that a high-quality service orientation is such a powerful competitive weapon that it will soon come to be regarded as an essential part of business strategy, not a frill or a "nice-to-have" feature. Organizations that cannot demonstrate a significant commitment to the needs of their customers will be left further and further behind. Quality of service is now a top-management issue.

And finally, the evidence from a number of successful organizations points to the concept of *managing the moments of truth* as the primary driving philosophy of service management. Service management is a far cry from the old "complaint department" approach. It is much more than "putting somebody in charge of service."

Service management is a top-down, whole-organization approach that starts with the nature of the customer's experience and creates strategies and tactics that maximize the quality of that experience. Service management means turning the whole organization into a customer-driven business entity, which is usually a very tall order.

Organizations that have achieved excellence in service are easy to spot, and their internal characteristics are fairly easy to identify. Our experience—as we have suggested throughout—shows that highly successful service organizations share at least the following characteristics:

1. They have a strong vision—a strategy for service that is clearly developed and clearly communicated.
2. They practice visible management.
3. They "talk" service routinely.
4. They have customer-friendly service systems.
5. They balance high-tech with high-touch, that is, they temper their systems and methods with the personal factor.
6. They recruit, hire, train, and promote for service.
7. They market service to their customers.
8. They market service internally, that is, to their employees.
9. They measure service and make the results available to the service people.

HOW TO TEACH AN ELEPHANT TO DANCE

The process of reorienting a large organization toward its market is analogous to trying to teach an elephant to dance. Many of the same challenges are involved. At least two things have to happen in order for an elephant to dance or for a large organization to change its ways. First, somebody has to show that it's possible to do so. Second, there must be a motivating factor sufficiently powerful to enlist commitment.

Service management offers a way to create and communicate a vision of service, and to make that vision a reality in the day-to-day business. In the sense of making an organization a customer-driven business entity, service management can be the means of teaching the elephant to dance.

THE FIVE STEPS TO A CUSTOMER-DRIVEN ORGANIZATION

When we look at the wide range of case examples of outstanding service organizations, we can discern a common thread that makes them more alike than different. There are certain distinctive common elements of service orientation, and there are some reliable guideposts that can help us along the road. As we have said previously, an organization is service-driven when it has a clear service strategy, customer-oriented frontline people, and customer-friendly systems for delivering its service.

Creating a new service orientation in an old-style organization usually involves some form of the following five stages:

1. Evaluating the present level of service quality.
2. Clarifying the service strategy.
3. Educating the organization.
4. Implementing new tactics at the front line.
5. Reinforcing the new orientation and making it permanent.

We shall explore each of these phases in greater depth.

STEP 1: THE SERVICE AUDIT—DISCOVERING THE REPORT CARD

The very first thing we have to do is to find out what's going on in the mind of the customer. This calls for a *service audit*, which is a thorough assessment of the interaction between the organization and the customer at all known points of contact. We want to discover what report card the customer presently has in mind, and what marks we have earned so far.

The particulars of a comprehensive service audit are too numerous to describe in detail here, so we will content ourselves with sketching the broad outlines of the process. In order to perform a valid service audit, we must start with a valid set of criteria for service quality. If we don't have valid criteria, we have no hope of making any kind of objective assessment. Our first order of business in such a case is to define or discover the necessary quality criteria.

To develop valid criteria for service quality, we need an intimate understanding of what our customers want and need from us. If we have been doing good market research on a regular basis, we will have all the information we need to help us understand the customer's expectations and motivations. If our market research is weak or nonexistent, however, then we must include at least a minimal study of customer demographics and psychographics as the first step in our service audit.

If the organization is in a fairly stable situation, with a relatively low rate of change in customer buying patterns and we have a fairly clear picture of customer expectations, then we can make the service audit a highly systematic process. However, if there is a great deal of upheaval or confusion in the market place, with rapidly changing customer satisfaction criteria, then the service audit may turn out to be a highly creative process.

Assuming a fairly well-defined service package, i.e., the combination of primary and secondary benefits we are offering the customer, it makes good sense to start the audit by studying the cycle—or cycles—of service our customers experience. We can diagram the various cycles of service that go on all over the organization. Having diagrammed all the cycles, we can then proceed to identify the moments of truth involved in each of them. Once we have this systematic framework for evaluating the situation, we can proceed to gather data in a fairly conventional way.

In a hospital, for example, we might want to subdivide the service package into a number of component packages we can evaluate separately. We might choose to distinguish between in-patient and out-patient services, for example. In each of these areas we could identify types of experiences our customer-patients might have, and the cycles of service that go along with each of them.

One cycle of service on the out-patient side might involve routine physical exams. We can trace the process from the time the customer makes contact with the scheduling office until he or she receives the final report of the exam. At each point there are moments of truth which we must evaluate.

The second step in the service audit is to decide what means to use in gathering the assessment data we need. Here we can choose among techniques, such as customer surveys, personal interviews or telephone interviews, and "focus group" interviews that include groups of customers who volunteer for feedback. We can also use the same data-gathering methods in asking questions of frontline service people in the organization. They can often provide facts and perspectives we might not know about.

Once we have sketched out the various cycles of service, identified the many moments of truth associated with them, and gathered measurement data on them, we are ready to compile the data and organize them in a form suitable for management discussion. We can spot the prominent gaps in our knowledge of customer expectations, identify the areas where we fall dangerously low in quality, and identify the areas where we shine. With this kind of profile of service quality, we are ready to attack the question: "What should our service strategy be?"

STEP 2: STRATEGY DEVELOPMENT—FIGURING OUT HOW TO GET HIGH MARKS

One of our favorite questions to ask executives is, "If you could get all the people in your organization to keep their minds on one single thing, what would it be?" Some executives can answer the question immediately, while others are stumped. The one who has an immediate and meaningful answer is usually one who has spent a great deal of time thinking about the process of communicating the strategy.

If the executive has no particular "message" to give to people at all levels of the organization, then they will probably keep their minds on a wide variety of things. The people may do the best jobs they can, but if they are left to their own best efforts, there will probably be relatively little synergy in their combined activities. By way of contrast, an effective service strategy provides the common focus that managers and workers need to help them maximize the quality of the customer's experience. It also provides the basis for a marketing campaign that can present a believable message to the customer.

How can we actually come up with an effective strategy? What do we do? One of the most effective methods for thinking through the strategy is the *executive retreat*. This is usually a special gathering of top managers for the sole purpose of analyzing the market research information and defining the organization's approach to customer service.

A typical executive retreat takes place at a meeting site remote from the day-to-day business. This may be a hotel conference room, a resort lodge that caters to business meetings, or a special conference facility. Usually the facility is comfortable, the dress is casual, and the atmosphere is one of informal but intensive work. Such a meeting might last for two or three days, with evening sessions if necessary. Meals are usually brief and informal, and there may be occasional breaks to relax and restore energy.

Many executives prefer to bring in a consultant or other highly skilled support person who is trained in group problem-solving techniques to facilitate the process of developing the strategy. They believe that the consultant's objective point of view and lack of any particular role bias enables that person to challenge their thinking and help them discover alternatives that may not have been obvious. In addition, some consultants are highly skilled in the use of creative thinking techniques that are not always familiar to the executives.

An effective retreat has several prerequisites. The first requirement is an atmosphere of open discussion and candid problem solving. The executives need to approach the process with the willingness to surface and deal with important issues. They must be willing to level with one another and to express their views freely.

Another requirement for success is an attitude of open-mindedness on the part of the individual executives. They must be willing to defer judgement on the various issues that arise, to listen for facts and points of view, and to look at various aspects of an issue before taking positions on it. It is important that a creative strategy retreat serve as a contest of ideas rather than a contest of personalities.

A third requirement for an effective retreat is a problem-solving process, or model, that all the participants can understand and apply. This requires careful thought and preparation. People who are unfamiliar with group dynamics, group problem solving, and the creative thinking process tend to approach a meeting that deals with complex issues with an attitude of "Let's get things settled." They may feel uncomfortable with a free-wheeling, divergent thinking process and insist on taking sides prematurely on key issues. Too often, such a meeting becomes a matter of battling with opinions. The person with the strongest voice, the biggest pile of computer printouts, or the highest rank may "win" the meeting, but that may not lead to long-term support and commitment.

With the right people present, the right atmosphere, and the right process, the group can proceed to examine the organization's current situation and prospects in light of the market research. This process should be a thorough, unhurried, in-depth analysis of the key facts, trends, questions, and issues. The executives need to review the current market environment, customer demographics and psychographics, competition, present image, past successes and failures, and possible avenues for positioning the organization competitively.

As the process unfolds, all participants must be willing to ask and answer some fundamental questions about the enterprise. What is our business? What really counts with the customer today? What will count tomorrow? What do the market research data tell us about the customer's real needs, motivational structure, and buying tendencies? Where is our real opportunity in the market? What can we do with our service that the customer will really notice and pay for?

Here are some other key questions: How does the customer see us at present? What are we best known for? In what ways do we excel? What image and role in the market would be plausible to our customers? How can we broaden our image in the customer's mind? How can we expand our range of action?

The aim of this highly creative process is to invent, discover, or evolve a service strategy that can unify the people of the organization. An effective service strategy is a statement of intent that meets at least the following conditions:

1. It is nontrivial; it has weight. It must be more than simply a "motherhood" statement or slogan. It must be reasonably concrete and action-oriented.
2. It must convey a concept or a mission which people in the organization can understand, relate to, and somehow put into action.
3. It must offer or relate to a critical benefit premise that is important to the customer. It must focus on something the customer is willing to pay for.
4. It must differentiate the organization in some meaningful way from its competitors in the eyes of the customer.
5. If at all possible, it should be simple, unitary, easy to put into words, and easy to explain to the customer.

Coming up with an effective service strategy is usually much more challenging and difficult than it first appears. Often the discussion of strategy may degenerate into platitudes about the goodness of the organization and pleas to the frontline people to work harder, smile harder, and be more thoughtful. This kind of diffused message generally leads to the "brass bands and armbands" approach we described previously. We can put buttons on the lapels of all employees, but if the buttons don't really say anything, not much will happen.

There are some notable examples of very concrete, specific service strategies which help frontline people keep their minds on the quality of the customer's experience. In the case of Deluxe Check Printers, Inc., the strategy is fairly simple: a fast turnaround on check-printing orders. Deluxe's management determined many years ago that a reliable, speedy response was all-important to banks who want to maintain a good service image with their new customers. If the checks come along weeks after the customer opens the account, the customer assumes the bank is slow and inefficient. So the gospel that Deluxe's executives preach and teach is the quick turnaround.

McDonald's Corporation, the hugely successful hamburger

chain, has a simple and easily taught service strategy: *fast* food, well prepared, and a consistent standard of quality.

Sears, Roebuck & Co. has for many years followed a money-back guarantee policy at their retail stores. This service strategy is so deeply ingrained in Sears's customers as well as the sales people that it has become virtually an article of faith. "If you're not satisfied with it, take it back and get a refund." Sears may have other problems with its image, but trust and reliability are not among them.

The Sharper Image, an up-scale mail-order firm located in San Francisco, has built a profitable business with a simple and consistent service strategy: high-quality products aimed at young, professional males who have money to spend and want to indulge themselves. Part of the strategy is a no-questions-asked money-back guarantee, which provides the element of trust that is absolutely critical in the direct-mail business.

A new service strategy usually calls for some degree of redirection of the organization. In some cases the strategy might be to hold course and speed, and continue to do what we do best. This calls for finding ways to do it better, and finding ways to communicate the priorities more strongly to the people of the organization.

On the other hand, a new strategy might call for reorienting the organization to its market and its customers. The executives may decide to change the mixture of services offered, to emphasize some services and deemphasize others, or to change the way in which the frontline people provide the services.

In an extreme situation, the executives may decide to make a radical change in the entire business position of the organization. A number of service organizations, such as churches, the Boy Scouts and Girl Scouts, and colleges, have found themselves dangerously out of touch with their "customers," perhaps because they never perceived them as customers. Most hospitals probably fall into this category—at least to some extent—and many of them are going through very troubled times trying to completely reposition themselves.

Under the service management concept, the outcome of the strategy formulation process is a declaration of competitive direction which becomes the organization's service gospel. It becomes the job of managers at all levels to preach and teach this gospel, and to help the people of the organization put it into practice.

STEP 3: EDUCATION—PREACHING AND TEACHING THE GOSPEL OF SERVICE

So far, we have spoken somewhat disparagingly of the inappropriate use of training as a means of improving the organization's service orientation. We have contended that a great deal of training in service industries really amounts to "smile training," i.e., trying to teach intelligent adults "how to be nice." Nevertheless, we have concluded from our experiences with large organizations as well as from the substantial evidence of successes in Europe, that well-designed, large-scale training programs can play a strong role in making an organization customer-driven.

Scandinavian Airlines trained more than 20,000 employees in an effort to revitalize the organization. British Airways trained over 37,000 people with the same objective. In both cases the program consisted of two full days of personal development training. The theory behind this large investment in human resources development was that helping people improve their personal life skills would make them more effective and productive in their jobs. Jan Carlzon of SAS and Colin Marshall of British Airways firmly believed in offering something of personal value to the employees instead of just putting them through a training program in "customer service."

"Mass training" of employees on the scale of SAS or British Airways is not a typical practice in American business, particularly in service industries. Many service employees receive little or no formal training, and have to pick up their skills as best they can through on-the-job experience. Rather than use mass training methods, the customary American approach to getting better frontline performance is usually to train the middle managers and perhaps the first-line supervisors in the basics of motivation and supervision.

The hope in such situations is that the concepts of good service will somehow trickle down through all the layers of the organization until they reach the performance-level people. Most executives realize, however, that complex concepts seldom trickle down very far. More typically, they fade out after passing through two or three levels.

Another part of the distinctly American approach of top-down implementation is to use formal job standards in an attempt to define specific behaviors on the part of frontline people that add up to "friendliness." This is especially appealing in industries that have highly programmed, repetitive job functions such as food service, retail sales, and hospitality. Yet there is good cause to question the effectiveness of purely top-down methods.

Imposing job standards from the top often leads to highly bureaucratic forms of management that fail to earn the commitment and enthusiasm of service people. They often feel insulted and pushed around when the supervisors start talking about measuring their performance and evaluating them on the basis of service behaviors. The implication seems to be that such employees have to be prodded into giving good service.

On the other hand, some observers of the Scandinavian scene have contended that simple mass training programs of the type used there merely serve to "hype" the organization, without creating a basis for lasting change. Although it seems that the top-down "legislative" approach has its drawbacks, mass training alone may not be the whole solution either.

A thoughtful combination of American approaches and those used in Scandinavia and other parts of Europe seems to hold promise for a new philosophy of service in the United States. We see this amalgam of methods as a combination of mass training, which is European in style, with planned evolution of the organization's culture, which is an approach more extensively developed by American companies than by European enterprises. Many U.S. companies, like Federal Express and Marriott Hotels, have a long tradition of effective service training. Others are catching on. Clearly, it is not enough just to train people. There has to be a follow-through process. The culture of the organization must reward and reinforce commitment, creative effort, and enthusiasm. The implementation of service management has to be a process of developing the whole organization. If we can do this, then training plays its natural role, management makes more sense, and the norms of the organization shift in the direction of customer consciousness.

STEP 4: IMPLEMENTATION—RELEASING CREATIVITY AT THE GRASS ROOTS

How do we get effective follow-through with a service management program or process? How can we implement the follow-through so it can survive, thrive, and grow? How can we gain the involvement and commitment of the majority of the people in the organization? These are the crucial questions facing us in the implementation stage. We need to find ways to help service people apply their energy and skills for the benefit of the customer and consequently for the benefit of the organization.

The most promising way to gain commitment is to put the problem of service quality squarely in the hands of the people who are performing the service. Instead of *telling* them in microscopic detail what service quality is and how to behave to produce it, we should *ask* them to define it for themselves. We should invite and challenge them to find ways of their own to maximize the quality of the customer's experience. Not only should we educate them in the ways of thinking about service, but we should also give them the freedom to develop effective service tactics by themselves. This relieves managers of the task of trying to specify behavior, and it releases a tremendous amount of creativity at the grass roots.

The quality circle is one mechanism for improving grass-roots effectiveness by enabling people to find better ways to do their jobs. In a service organization, the quality circle can become a service circle. It can provide a basis for investigation, problem solving, and innovation, and for developing new methods of meeting customer needs.

Briefly defined, a quality circle is a group of working-level people who meet on a regular basis to find better ways to do their work. A typical quality circle is an intact work group—although there can be exceptions to this general rule. The group supervisor usually serves as the leader of the circle. In some organizations quality circles work with trained facilitators who show the workers problem-solving methods and help them apply the methods to improve the products or services they provide.

British Airways has used service circles as a fundamental part of its implementation strategy, both in Britain and abroad. Following through on chief executive Colin Marshall's gospel of "putting the customer first," the company has created over 70 service circles at home and over 40 in other countries. These circles have produced thousands of recommendations and ideas for improvement; hundreds of these ideas have been implemented and have resulted in noticeable improvements in either the quality of service or in cost savings.

The service circle method may prove especially beneficial in the United States because so many companies have had experience with quality circles. Not all of them have made effective use of the circles, and not all have been completely satisfied, but the quality circle concept offers much promise. When quality circles go off the track, it is frequently because they lack a focus of attention. Groups may spend too much time on side issues like the food in the company cafeteria, and managers may find the results underwhelming.

Giving quality circles a service mission can put them back on a more rewarding track. Looking for new and better ways to score high marks on the customer's report card can give the group a sense of importance and a feeling that it is making a worthwhile contribution to the organization's success. In turn, this can foster a sense of excitement, commitment, and renewed enthusiasm that can carry the service management program through.

STEP 5: MAINTENANCE—MAKING SERVICE COMMITMENT A WAY OF LIFE

Once the service management program is well under way in our organization, and assuming it is beginning to "take" with the people, the next step is to start building organizational structures that will help it become permanent. This can often be the sticking point of the whole process because sacred cows usually die hard. It is quite common to find organizational customs, traditions, policies, systems, procedures, and work rules that stand in the way of new and creative service methods. Enthusiastic employees who have good ideas can quickly become discouraged by the layers of bureaucracy, red tape, and "can'ts" that seem to assail them at every turn.

Few managers will admit to being bureaucratic in their methods, and almost all of them will agree with the need for creative new approaches. But when the time comes to change their own ways of doing things, the difference between "theory" and "practice" emerges. People in organizations can become amazingly attached to their current habits and procedures. This is a stage at which top management's attention and influence can play an important role. If the executives remind managers at all levels of the importance of the service strategy, and kindly but firmly encourage them to support it in practice, it is possible to break through the fossilized structures of habit. New and more effective ways can replace the old ways.

Implementing a service management program in a large organization calls for a strong education process, as previously discussed, and it also calls for continuing management support. Managers need to be visible and consistent in their support for the service concept. They need to embrace their roles in preaching and teaching the gospel of service, and they should pay special attention to reinforcing the service orientation on the part of performance-level people.

And finally, as the service management process matures, it becomes appropriate to make sure that support systems in the organization are aligned to the service concept. For example, does the recruiting and hiring process attract people who can fulfill service roles effectively? Does the orientation program for new employees instill the service strategy in their minds right from the start? Does the company newsletter preach the same gospel that the chief executive preaches? Do the training programs advance the cause of effective service? Does the performance planning system actualize the goals of the service management program? Does the appraisal system provide feedback to employees about the effectiveness of their efforts?

At some indistinguishable point, the service management program ceases to be a program and becomes the basic orientation of the organization. Getting to that point may involve a large investment of time, energy, money, and creative thinking. The organizations that make that investment most effectively will be the ones that thrive and grow.

AVOID THESE MISTAKES

Implementing the service management concept in a large organization seems straightforward in concept. In fact, it is so simple in concept that many managers are tempted to underestimate the magnitude of the task. Changing the culture of a group of people is anything but easy. It is seldom simple, and it is almost never quick. Unfortunately, managers who are enthusiastic and action-oriented often try to advance by the most direct route, often with disappointing results.

It is a capital mistake, for example, to underestimate the crucial effect employee attitudes can have on the success of any such program. A group of people who are burned out, turned off, cynical, demoralized, or who suffer from any combination of these problems can simply fail to buy in to the spirit of the campaign. For this reason it is usually a good idea to assess the climate of the organization at the outset. By conducting employee surveys, interviews, and focus groups, we can determine the levels of morale, optimism, and energy we will encounter during the implementation period.

Not only must we have the support, or at least the readiness of the people in the organization, we must also have a program that makes sense. It must appeal to people on a number of levels, from head to heart. As a final observation about implementing service management, we offer from our experience a short list of ways to do it wrong. Here are some of the most common mistakes, or traps, that we have seen managers fall into in trying to carry out large campaigns to reorient their organizations. May you never be guilty of any of them.

Short attention span. Top management gets all fired up, but by the time the posters come back from the print shop, they are distracted by other "more pressing" problems and forget what they had set out to do. This is the "theme-of-the-month" style that creates cynicism among the working people of the organization and destroys whatever credibility the executives may have enjoyed in their eyes. It is important to get into the game for the long run, and to make up the collective management mind to stay the course.

Empty slogans. Lacking a real strategy for service, and not knowing how to arrive at one, some management groups resort to advertising slogans to try to hoodwink the customer into believing that something has changed. An empty slogan is harmless at best, and sometimes it simply wastes some money. But it can often backfire, especially if the actual level of service quality is far less than the commercial implies. The slogans should come only after we truly have something to brag about that will make a difference to the customer.

Brass bands and armbands. The brass band approach is the internal version of the advertising slogan approach. It is an attempt to hype the service employees without having a strategy to preach or teach. Lapel buttons, posters, and motivational films do little for service quality unless your employees know what the customer appeal needs to be, and know how to deliver it. Let's make the message a meaningful one. Let's develop a competitive service strategy and take that message, not hype, to the people.

Smile training. By all means let's use training. Dollar for dollar, it can be an excellent payoff. Who knows but one critical moment of truth, handled skillfully by someone in whose development we have invested our money, might have an enormous impact on the customer's evaluation of our organization? But let's not insult our employees with smile training or "be nice" training. Let's treat them like adults and give them the tools and the information that will help them figure out how to handle their moments of truth effectively.

Rigor mortis. Administratively-minded managers sometimes find it tempting to overorganize the service management process. By creating paper systems, forms, reports, procedures, review committees, and all the other trappings of overcontrol, they can strangle the process before it ever gets healthy. Let's use an organized campaign-type approach, but let's keep the focus on individual contributions and service quality.

12

Service Tomorrow: What Can We Expect?

> We look forward optimistically to the next decade: services of all
> kinds will get better and better.
> —*Karl Albrecht/Ron Zemke*

Will service be as important a part of our economic tomorrow
as it is today? No. It will be *more* important. By all indications
the increasing shift from industrial America to service America,
the demand for more and better services, and the increasing number of service jobs will make us all much more service-conscious.
This will happen not only in the United States but also all around
the developed world.

This book is not only about service America. You could replace
"America" with the name of any of the other developed countries
and the title would still have the same meaning.

Some analysts suggest that by the year 2000, which is not
very far away, as many as 88 percent of the American work force
will be engaged in service jobs. Do you find that hard to believe?
Try this simple test. Open your checkbook and scan the check
register. There you'll get an idea of the broad range of services
that already touch your everyday life: dry cleaning, a hair cut,
insurance, flowers, movie tickets, a restaurant tab, a charge card
payment, the plumber, new eyeglasses, a pizza, the babysit-
ter, postage stamps, health club fees, television repairs, a car
tune-up, and an oil change.

RISING EXPECTATIONS

People are becoming much more conscious of the mediocre levels
of service they receive in many aspects of their lives, and they
are getting mad about it. They want to see something done to
improve this situation. Ironically, part of what is making them

mad is seeing that excellent service is possible and profitable for the best companies; they want more of what they see.

We can look forward optimistically to living in the next decade for a very good reason: services of all kinds will get better and better. The movement to a service economy and a service culture is so strong, so glacial in its character, that it will be a driving force in the competitive arena of business for many years. Our progressive expectations as customers and the creativity of those who want our business will set ever higher standards of what is acceptable in service.

In the short run, perhaps over the next two to three years, we will probably see an energetic commitment to advertising and promotion by service organizations. Initially it will be a battle of platitudes. Competitors will vie with one another for the niftiest, most creative slogans that tell how customer-oriented they are.

During this early period, probably only about 10 to 15 percent of the players will really be able to swing their organizational cultures around to make them truly customer-driven. The other companies will continue to invent slogans, hoping that the right advertising message will do the trick. As the service philosophy becomes more and more fundamental to doing business, the other companies will gradually figure out how to do it, too.

Traditional services may become more personal in nature, even as some other services become "industrialized" and less personal. For every automatic teller machine that does away with an interpersonal transaction, there may be an increasing personal involvement in, say, automobile repair. Naisbitt's high-tech/high-touch idea seems to come back again and again.

THERE IS PLENTY OF ROOM FOR INNOVATION

We will also see entirely new services come into existence. As we become more demanding in our role as service buyers, providers will become more creative in their offerings. Here are just a few samples of novel services we are seeing:

- *Computer mating for dollars*—not young lovers are involved here, but young businesses seeking capital. Venture Capital Network, for example, uses a computer data base and a telecommunications hookup to match new companies with venture capitalists.
- *Fast food delivery*—not just pizza, but just about anything

that can "travel." It is the corner pizza delivery service gone generic.

- *House sitting with a guarantee*—when a company provides a sitter, they provide insurance and minimize the risk of damage. Some are using retired people at minimum cost. They also take good care of dogs, cats, and plants.
- *Kids only shops*—book stores, for example, that cater only to young children and carry only children's books.
- *Shop-for-me services*—the growth of the two-person household has opened up opportunities for people who hunt down clothing, furniture, vacations, and a variety of other services.
- *Software search*—personal computer users face such a time-consuming and tedious task in finding and evaluating software for their needs that special search services are springing up to help them.
- *Temporary help*—the temporary-help business isn't just for typists and day labor any longer. Professional accountants, computer programmers, rented executives—you name it.

Sometimes new services come into being as a way to eliminate other services that cost a great deal. John Naisbitt refers to this phenomenon as *bypassing*. For example, teleconferencing and personal computer link ups over the telephone can reduce the need for air travel. The coming of the computer may reduce the dependence on formal public education structures. Even electrical power generation by public utilities may give ground to some extent to "co-generation," that is, the cooperative generation of electrical power from waste heat created by manufacturing processes.

THE NEWLY DEREGULATED EVERYTHING

Deregulation of major American industries will also present big opportunities for companies that can move with the times. Many Europeans are shocked at the nature and speed of deregulation in the United States. "How," they ask, "can the United States possibly survive with its major public services—health care, transportation, communications, and who knows what next—freed to succeed or fail at the will of the marketplace? What about the public interest?"

Telecommunications is a classic example. We've referred to the problems of the new AT&T several times, and the regional phone companies have made their share of headlines since divestiture.

But the fact is that the phones in America still work, and they work better than the phones in most other countries. Companies like MCI and Sprint are coming up with new rates and services, and promises that we won't be sorry that the old Ma Bell is no more.

Questions persist, however. The competition seems to be spending as much time in front of the rate commissions as the old Bell companies did. And although the phones are still ringing, many people are wondering whether we will really see the decreased rates and increased innovation promised to us as a rationale for the breakup.

Critic Alexander Cogburn is most blunt: "A once proud company is now desperately shoveling technological junk onto the market, and is still battling with deregulation. Of course it is battling. If you sawed the tail off a kangaroo and told it to be a greyhound, the wretched thing would have problems, too."

An internal memorandum at AT&T, circulated before the breakup, admonished employees to remember that, as of January 1, 1984, they would no longer be in the "service" business. On that score Boston University's Stanley Davis comments: "Universal service *was* at the core of AT&T's culture, and they have foolishly abandoned it instead of redefining it." A recent rash of service-centered advertisements suggest that AT&T may indeed be returning to what it has always known best—making it simple and easy for people to "reach out and touch someone."

While the industry is in upheaval and heading for some sort of a competitive shake-up, who is helping the consumer understand what is going on? Certainly not the courts and public commissions. Thanks to them, our monthly phone bills look like phone books. Since the employees of AT&T are confused about their mission and franchise, and since customers are just plain tired of the telephone shuffle, there has to be a great growth opportunity for whoever can write a clean chapter in the history of telecommunications. Meanwhile, no one is completely happy with today's telecommunications services.

Banking isn't a newly deregulated industry, but it comes close to being one. The "financial supermarket" is becoming increasingly popular with consumers, and competition is increasingly keen. While banks are offering "nonbanking" services, companies like Sears Financial Network, American Express subsidiaries IDS and Shearson, and Merrill Lynch, Pierce, Fenner & Smith, Inc., are learning to offer services formerly reserved for banks.

The big issue in banking and financial services is "turf." The large money center banks like Citibank, Chase Manhattan, and Bank of America have become a threat to the once secure regional banks. They capitalize on increasingly flexible interpretations of the federal banking regulations that allow major banks to compete on an interstate basis through credit card and telebanking services.

The whole financial services community is finding out that when the competition is intense, good service counts just as much as attractive products and name recognition. Susan Richards, a Chicago-area financial services consultant, puts it nicely: "The bottom line of all this is that competition in the 1980s will revolve around pricing and service. Marketing and expanded customer services will become the key to surviving the rest of the decade."

Transportation, on the ground and in the air, is going through the same trauma of deregulation. The air travel customer, for example, can choose from a range of options ranging between coast-to-coast luxury flights with gourmet meals and superlow-cost "no frills" flights. So far, only the latter seem to be profitable.

Train travel is a candidate for some innovative approaches. While the trains can never offer the speed and convenience of air travel, there are many people who would prefer the more relaxed, less hectic, and more "civilized" experience of riding a train to their destination. The government-supported Amtrak organization has, however, not displayed a trace of imagination or innovative thinking in its approach to the customer.

Airlines will probably begin moving toward the "total travel" concept. Scandinavian Airlines is a frontrunner in this movement. SAS has recognized that people don't just "fly," they take trips, and taking a trip involves much more than traveling on an airplane. The company plans to move into the hotel business, the tour business, and a variety of other areas connected logically with its core business of air travel.

Many international air carriers and hotel companies have their eyes on the potentially huge China travel market. They drool as they think about the rapid increase in tourist travel to China and the potential for flying, feeding, housing, and touring huge numbers of people as China becomes the "in" place to visit.

Health care is a business undergoing a devastating revolution. We hesitate to call it an industry at this point because it is emerging from a period of unprecedented favored status in American life. Health care has been a seller's market for so long that the people in it have had no concept of competition, marketing, pricing, or promotion. The wrenching changes that have hit health care in the last five years have caused confusion, pain, and a very late awakening.

A steady decline in the average length of a hospital stay, combined with the buying influence of major third-party payers like Blue Cross and the Federal government, and "capitated" systems of reimbursement for treatment (based on fixed per-person payments regardless of the details of the case) have forced doctors and hospitals to hustle for business.

Hospital-based health care delivery may be going the way of the house call. The cost of maintaining a hospital that isn't full of patients is astronomical, and virtually every large city in the country is oversupplied with hospitals and beds. Hospitals are going out of business at the rate of one a week, and that number is accelerating.

Doctors as high-status, high-income professionals are taking a fall. It may turn out to be just as hard a fall as attorneys have taken. The prospect of a physician advertising on television for patients may seem bizarre, but the prospect of a lawyer doing it was equally bizarre ten years ago before the legal field got overcrowded. In a recent questionnaire survey we conducted among physicians, 37 percent of them expressed the intention of using "marketing methods" in promoting their practices. Another 25 percent were undecided at the time of the survey.

Health-maintenance organizations—HMOs—offer attractive features for buyers and sellers of health services alike. A person signs up for an HMO membership, pays a single monthly fee, and receives all the care he or she needs from a system consisting of doctors, clinics, medical treatment resources, and usually a hospital. The doctors and the hospital benefit because the HMO structure includes a marketing and promotion program, and the HMO is a source of patients. This provides a respectable way for physicians to market themselves.

As the health care market becomes more turbulent, more and more innovative options for service appear. For example, the freestanding emergency center, sometimes called the emergi-center, or ambulatory care center, is a walk-in facility where people can obtain immediate care, and not necessarily only for emergencies. Many physicians and hospital executives complain that these "doc-in-a-box" businesses are "creaming" the top of the market, but it's an everyone-for-himself situation. Anything that is legal, ethical, and profitable will probably be tried.

At this stage hospitals are sitting ducks for being bypassed by some sort of innovative "leapfrog" maneuver, possibly even by hotels or similar businesses. Marriott Hotels' move into the residential elder care business is but a first incursion. Hospitals could end up in a declining, obsolescent mode—much like the railroads after the advent of air travel—if they don't find new ways to serve their customers. As the number of patients drops, most hospital executives simply respond passively by cutting back on services and laying off employees. There is a limit to the value of this habitual response, and the limit is the point at which the hospitals can no longer adapt or compete.

IMPORTING AND EXPORTING SERVICES

One exciting avenue for the future, which may offer great promise to American service companies, is the export of services. We traditionally think of only hard goods as being exportable, but in fact we have been exporting services for a long time. The Hilton, Marriott, and Sheraton hotel chains operate successfully in other countries. American Express is an internationally known service company.

Other industries, like the airlines, are moving to establish a stronger foothold in developing markets, such as the Chinese market mentioned above. Architect-engineering firms, such as those that build large factories, refineries, and public development projects, will see more and more opportunity for their work.

As the United States continues to lose the competitive edge in "smokestack" industries, and sees those industries steadily migrating outward to the low-labor-cost countries, we can continue to maintain an edge in two key areas: technology and service. At this point American companies enjoy a fairly strong advantage in technology, with Japanese firms breathing down their necks.

Service, however, is another matter. While no other country is generally credited with the ability to outclass American service, the United States does not enjoy an undisputed reputation for service. We will have to earn such a reputation. It can be done, but it will take hard work, commitment, investment, and enlightened management.

MANAGEMENT IS A SERVICE, TOO

We would like to wrap up our message with one final thought: doing business in the new economy will require new ways of managing. The days are fast fading when managers can deal with employees from totalitarian, authority-based roles. The traditional approach to motivation, which management theorist Frederick Herzberg calls "management by K.I.T.A.—kick in the ass"—simply doesn't work in a setting that involves thousands or millions of moments of truth every day. We must find ways to make service quality worthwhile and important to the people who do the service.

Just as we can't legislate "friendliness," we can't legislate motivation, commitment, or creativity either. A person working in a service role has a tremendous amount to give—both to the customer and the organization. We must teach our managers to invite that generosity, to appreciate it, and to reward it. Service quality is all about values, expectations, norms for behavior, and rewards; in short, it is all about culture. We must create and maintain organizational cultures that make quality possible and worthwhile.

We believe a new philosophy of management is beginning to take shape in the United States in response to the need for more creative ways to think about, organize for, and deliver service. This new philosophy will emphasize greater top-management involvement and leadership, decentralized control of service standards, supportive organizational cultures, and willingness to realign organizational structures to meet the needs of the customer more effectively.

This new point of view suggests that we had better start looking at the very process of management itself as a service. The most important question the manager can ask of the performance-level person is, "What can I do that will help you get your job done better?"

Olle Stiwenius, director of Scandinavian Airlines management consultants, says, "I think it's time we turned the 'pyramid' upside down. We need to put management at the bottom, in a supporting role. If you draw the diagram that way, you start to think about words like 'support,' 'facilitate,' and 'balance.' This gets managers to think about their responsibilities in a completely new way."

Futurist John Naisbitt says much the same thing:

> During the last few years we have witnessed the beginning of the transformation of the U.S. corporation. . . . The shift [is] from managers who traditionally were supposed to have all the answers and tell everyone what to do, to managers whose role it is to create a nourishing environment for personal growth. Increasingly we will think of managers as teachers, mentors, developers of human potential. . . . The challenge will be to re-train managers, not workers, for the re-invented, information-age corporation.[1]

We have found exemplars of good service management in virtually every industry. These are organizations with management teams that have mastered one or more of the key aspects of the art of service design, development, and delivery. At the same time this new service economy is just now unfolding. There are problems, challenges, and opportunities for even the most experienced.

As more and more managers start thinking of their jobs as service jobs, and finding ways to serve the needs of the people in their organizations, the factor of service quality will emerge more and more strongly as a competitive weapon. Organizations that have not moved beyond the traditional top-down modes of leadership will be more and more rigid and unable to adapt. Without a believable strategy for service, they will be left behind. We believe that those organizations that succeed in internalizing the philosophy of service management and building customer-driven cultures will flourish.

NOTES

CHAPTER 1

1. Russell Ackoff, Paul Broholm, and Roberta Snow, *Revitalizing Western Economies* (San Francisco: Jossey-Bass, 1984), p. 2.

   Ackoff et al. take issue with Naisbitt and others who use the term *postindustrial* to describe the current economy, and who spring from there to the argument that the shift in the economy's population base is from industrial to informational. They argue that postindustrial connotes the demise of industry rather than a shift in the employment base, which is clearly much more to the case. They further argue that for Naisbitt and others to be correct, the shift in employment would have to be toward jobs directly involved with information technology. This, according to all available statistics, is not the case. The data that exist clearly show that the employment shift in all of the more developing countries of the world is away from employment in manufacturing and toward employment in services. But there is also an equivocation to be observed; "Nevertheless, the changes occurring in both goods-producing and service industries are largely due to technological developments relating to the generation, processing, transmission, storage, and retrieval of information, particularly the microprocessor." Their point should not be lost. On the whole, most of the new jobs being created in the United States today are in the service sector and *not* directly related to information manipulation.

2. Several good books and essays make this point. The most critical is by Barbara Tuchman, "The Decline of Quality," *New York Times Magazine,* November 2, 1980. A nice photo essay on the same subject was by Jeremy Man, "Toward Service without a Snarl," *Fortune,* March 3, 1981. You have to overlook a bit of "one-simply-can't-get-good-help" snobbishness in these laments for service quality, but they do make their point.

3. The Arthur Andersen & Co. study was a Delphic forecast effort that went 2 rounds and involved 100 people split into 4 panels— 25 service industry people, 25 business planners, 25 technology mavens, and 25 customers–DP and telecommunications executives. The report is available for $100 a copy from the Association of Field Service Managers, 7273 President Court, Fort Meyer, FL 33902.

   The report doesn't suggest that primary providers of computer service, the manufacturers, are about to get completely out of that part of the business. These providers "must keep offering service as part of their sales and marketing strategy," regardless of how minimal and shoddy that service may be.

   A friend of ours recently regaled us with the trials and tribulations she was experiencing trying to get a fix on a microcomputer hard disk storage device. It seems that the dealer who talked her into buying it and who, coincidentally, advertises the fact that he has factory-trained technicians, had no one on staff qualified to service it. "A marginal product for us," the store manager told her, as if an understanding of his economics was going to convince her that the repair of this very expensive paperweight was not his problem. Frustrated on her first attempt at a remedy, our friend called the manufacturer. There she was told that she couldn't expect the manufacturer to deal with her problem—they were much too busy for that. "Go back to the dealer you bought it from," she was told. "The dealer won't help me," she replied. "Then you're in tough shape, Sweetie." Click! Eventually someone at the seller's store, who had experienced the same problem and solved it for himself, was able to repair the unit. But the damage was done. When the time came for our friend's department to plunge into full computerization, her horror story raised enough hackles that the offending equipment was considered too risky for adoption, and the dealer— despite a 25 percent corporate discount policy—was classified as too unreliable a supplier. Oh yes, that particular piece of hardware has recently joined the ranks of the orphaned. It is word of mouth like this that keeps some of us snug as a bug in the Apple/IBM rug.

4. Technical Assistance Research Programs Inc., (TARP) is located in Washington, D.C. if you are interested in more of their data, and there is certainly a lot more of it than we have shared with you here. They have done extensive work on a number of consumer satisfaction issues and their dollars-and-cents implications. They have studied the value of word of mouth in the soft drink industry, the use of 800 numbers as a consumer satisfaction tool, and the role of consumer satisfaction in automobile and auto parts purchase and repurchase.

The TARP formula for profits from complaint handling is an interesting exercise in logic. You buy the assumptions and you will be happy with the way they come to the conclusion that a satisfied consumer is worth a lot of money.

Profit = Long-term profits from loyal customer
+ Word of mouth
+ Regulatory response cost avoided
− Cost of handling

The half-million dollar figure was derived from data developed for the Clairol Corporation, not from P & G. The key variables are a five-year purchase history, 70 percent loyality rate for satisfied customer complaints, one new sale for every complaint favorably handled, a $500 cost or regulatory response, a 1:200 complaint to an agency rate, and administrative costs of $5.50 for each company responded to.

5. Ibid.

6. Ronald Kent Shelp, John C. Stephenson, Nancy Sherwood Truitt, and Bernard Wasow, *Service Industries and Economic Development*, (New York: Praeger Publishers, 1985), p. 3. Ron Shelp is an insurance executive who is one of the leading authorities on the role of services in the world economy. Several federal administrations have appointed him to commissions on services industries. Maybe he can get them to drop the system of classifying 60 percent of the GNP under the meaningless rubric of "services."

7. Ibid., pp. 4–5. Actually, the stages we describe are derived or adapted from Shelp; his description is focused on the needs of developing nations today. The problem he looks at is a good one. How can a developing or less developed nation move toward a well-managed service sector without repeating the stages Western countries have trekked through? This is no idle question in the face of the possibility that time and technology won't allow developing countries to take that route.

8. Theodore Levitt, "After the Sale Is Over . . . ," *Harvard Business Review* (September-October 1983), pp. 88–89. An important point here is that Levitt is not talking about the idea of relationship selling. Relationship selling has been a buzz phrase in the sales and sales training game for many years. What Levitt describes is relationship building between the buying *organization* and the selling *organization*. This is a more involved process than relationship selling, which can be loosely translated as, "Make the purchasing agent like you, and he'll buy from you." Perhaps the most descriptive phrase would be relationship marketing, the thrust of which is to form a long-

term liason with the customer rather than make a single sale. Reprinted by permission of *Harvard Business Review*. Excerpt from "After the sale is over . . ." by the President and Fellows of Harvard College; all rights reserved.

9. Ibid., p. 87.

10. Probably the most instructive reading on the topic of new respectability for service sector companies is a pair of *Fortune* magazine articles—"Ten Years of Bounding Profits," June 11, 1984, which features profiles of the most successful Fortune Service 500 companies and compares their overall results with the more dismal performance of the Fortune Industrial 500 list. The second article is "Corporate Stars that Brightened a Dark Decade," April 30, 1984. Here we are treated to the stories of 13 companies that had an average 20 percent ROE for the 10 years 1974–1983. Number two on the list, Dow Jones & Company, Inc., is a service company, but more interesting is the fact that 8 of the 13 are organizations with a strong service reputation in their home industry.

CHAPTER 2

1. American readers may not fully appreciate the strength of union involvement in company operations in Scandinavian countries. Swedish labor law requires full disclosure of all company financial matters, and consultation with union representatives *prior* to any major management initiative that might affect workers en masse. In a nutshell, the law requires that union leaders have access to all of the same information that is available to management. This, of course, is quite different from the situation in the States.

CHAPTER 6

1. F. Stewart DeBruicker and Gregory L. Summe, "Make Sure Your Customers Keep Coming Back," *Harvard Business Review* (January-February 1985), p. 92. Essentially DeBruicker and Summe argue that the world moves on. OK, that's obvious, but we seldom account for that simple fact in our business plans. Their argument presses home an important point: staying close to the customer isn't an every other Friday afternoon affair. It is an all-day, everyday part of the business. Take your eye off the ball and somebody will steal it.

2. Richard Normann, *Service Management: Strategy and Leadership in Service Businesses* (New York: John Wiley & Sons, 1984), p. 26. Normann is one of the first Europeans to work with the service management concept. He was associated with the SAS project and has been a leader making the East-West connection—frequently translating American thinking to the European context.

3. G. Lynn Shostack, "Designing Services That Deliver," *Harvard Business Review* (January-February 1984), p. 135.

4. Normann, *Service Management,* p. 15.

5. Shostack, "Designing Services," p. 137. Shostack credits the basics of the blueprint approach to the grand master of quality, W. Edwards Deming.

6. Ibid., p. 137.

CHAPTER 7

1. Vijay Sathe, "Implications of Corporate Culture: A Manager's Guide to Action," *Organizational Dynamics* (Autumn 1983), p. 8.

2. This is the opening paragraph of Gerstner's congratulations speech to the grand prize winners at the December 1983 Great Performers Awards luncheon. According to an Am Ex spokesperson, hundreds of employees are nominated for the awards every year. Of the episodes submitted, six get the grand prize money plus a four-day trip to the head office in New York City. Another five employees get a letter of commendation and a check for $1000.

3. For a detailed discussion of quality of work life and its measurement, see Karl Albrecht, *Organization Development: A Total Systems Approach to Positive Change in Any Business* (Englewood Cliffs, N.J.: Prentice-Hall, 1983).

CHAPTER 9

1. Giving credit where credit is due, this was a joint project with Wilson Learning Corporation, and their very proficient studios shot the video. The entire project has been written up as "Organization-Wide Intervention" by Ronald E. Zemke and John W. Gunkler in Lee Frederiksen, ed., *Handbook of Organizational Behavior Management* (New York: John Wiley & Sons, 1982), pp. 565–83.

2. Philip Crosby, *Quality without Tears* (New York: McGraw-Hill, 1984), p. 201.

3. Theodore Levitt, "After the Sale Is Over . . . ," *Harvard Business Review* (September-October 1983), pp. 88–89.

4. Richard J. Matteis, "The New Back Office Focuses on Customer Service," *Harvard Business Review,* (March-April 1979), pp. 128–42.

5. Philip Crosby, *Quality Is Free* (New York: McGraw-Hill, 1979), p. 173.

6. Zemke and Gunkler in Frederikson, ed., *Handbook of Behavior.* The idea of the well-defined business proposition as the start of a measurement system is explained in the research report from the theme park case in Chapter 10.

7. Crosby, *Quality Is Free, p. 203.*

CHAPTER 10

1. Carol J. Loomis, "Corporate Stars That Brightened a Dark Decade," *Fortune,* April 30, 1984, p. 153.

2. Stanley M. Davis, *Managing Corporate Culture* (Cambridge, Mass.: Ballinger Publishing Company, 1984), p. 1. Davis uses the word culture in a very specific way. "The pattern of shared beliefs and values that gives the members of an institution meaning, and provides them with the rules for their behavior in their organization. Every organization will have its own word or phrase to describe what it means by culture; some of these are: being, core, culture, ethos, identity, ideology, manner, patterns, philosophy, purpose, roots, spirit, style, vision, and way. To most managers these mean pretty much the same thing."

3. Ibid., p. 7.

4. F. Stewart DeBruicker and Gregory L. Summe, "Make Sure Your Customers Keep Coming Back," *Harvard Business Review*, (January/February 1985), pp. 92–98.

CHAPTER 12
1. John Naisbitt, *The Year Ahead: "These Ten Trends Will Shape the Way You Live, Work, and Make Money in 1985,"* (Washington, D.C.: The Naisbitt Group, 1985), p. 5.

BIBLIOGRAPHY

ACKOFF, RUSSELL L.; PAUL BROHOLM; AND ROBERTA SNOW. *Revitalizing Western Economies.* San Francisco: Jossey-Bass, 1985.

ALBRECHT, KARL. *Organization Development: A Total Systems Approach to Positive Change in Any Business.* Englewood Cliffs, N.J.: Prentice-Hall, 1983.

DAVIS, STANLEY M. *Managing Corporate Culture.* Cambridge, Mass.: Ballinger Publishing Company, 1984.

LEVINSON, HARRY, AND STUART ROSENTHAL. *CEO: Corporate Leadership in Action.* New York: Basic Books, 1984.

NAISBITT, JOHN. *Megatrends: Ten New Directions Transforming Our Lives.* New York: Warner Books, 1982.

NORMANN, RICHARD. *Service Management: Strategy and Leadership in Service Businesses.* New York: John Wiley & Sons, 1984.

"Office Automation and the Workplace." Minneapolis, Minn.: Honeywell, 1983.

PETERS, THOMAS J. AND ROBERT H. WATERMAN, JR. *In Search of Excellence.* New York: Harper & Rowe, 1982.

PETERS, THOMAS J. AND NANCY AUSTIN. *A Passion For Excellence.* New York: Random House, 1985.

SASSER, W. EARL, ED. *Service Management.* Boston, Mass.: Harvard Business Review Reprints, 1979.

SHELP, RONALD KENT; JOHN C. STEPHENSON; NANCY SHERWOOD TRUITT; AND BERNARD WASOW. *Service Industries and Economic Development.* New York: Praeger Publishers, 1984.

SMITH, HAROLD T. *The Office Revolution.* Willow Grove, Penn.: Administrative Management Society Foundation, 1983.

Statistical Abstracts of the United States; 1982–83. Washington, D.C.: U.S. Department of Commerce, 1983.

TOFFLER, ALVIN. *Future Shock.* New York: Random House, 1970.

————. *The Third Wave.* New York: William Morrow & Co., 1980.

1985 U.S. Industrial Outlook. Washington, D.C.: U.S. Department of Commerce, 1985.

ZEMKE, RONALD E., AND JOHN W. GUNKLER. "Organization-Wide Intervention." In *Handbook of Organizational Behavior Management,* ed. Lee Frederiksen. New York: John Wiley & Sons, 1982.

ZEMKE, RONALD E., AND THOMAS J. KRAMLINGER. *Figuring Things Out: A Trainer's Guide to Task and Needs Analysis.* Reading, Mass.: Addison-Wesley, 1982.

Index